Introduction

Various bibles present this passage of the deaf man gaining the ability to hear in different ways. In all of them there is a repeating sequence of all the "ands" Jesus does for the man to hear. But is that all that has been opened? Personally, I have come to believe that man was to hear in more than human form? Why is there emphasis on looking up to heaven and speaking the Aramaic "Ephphatha?"

Why is it necessary to repeat the translation into "that is, be opened"? Isn't possible that beside the human need to hear, Jesus is inviting heaven and divinity to be opened to the man. Isn't it possible that when we read the story we become that man and our own deafness to what is normally beyond our understanding is "opened?" This is not the only time Jesus lets us know that heaven is opened and all of divinity is available if we are willing to listen with our heart. His words are always filled with divine love for us, we just need open ourselves to receive them. Further still, being able to listen is only one half of communication. What of our own ability to participate with Christ's love on earth as it is in heaven?

One way to allow this love to daily wash over us is to use the practice of Lectio Divina (Divine Reading). Lectio is an ancient prayer technique originating with the church fathers that was further explored and adopted by the Benedictines and many others. Lectio is a way of allowing the Holy Spirit to illuminate and teach by way of personalizing Scripture. There are variations of Lectio but for the most part it consists of progressively reading, praying and reflecting on a Scripture passage.

The passage is first read then meditated on (Meditatio). A particular word, phrase, or concept may come to mind during this time. While not necessary, this insight can be a foundation for the next re-reading of the passage. The passage is read a second time followed by communicative prayer (Oratio) with the Trinity. Different prayer styles can be used such as having a silent conversation about the passage, insight, image, or concept that came to mind with God. The passage is read a third time followed by contemplative (Contemplatio) silence with God. During this time, we allow ourselves to be attentive and open to what God may want to communicate with/to us. On occasion, through grace, we may be invited into an even deeper union with

God for a short period.

Lectio gives us an opportunity to leverage the same faith as the deaf man which is to uniquely hear God's thoughts for us without hearing. In silence, we can hear what God has to uniquely say to us. Additionally, Lectio provides an understanding of scripture within the context of Jesus' desire for us to live in peace, love, hope, and faith.

Personally, I have found that prior to entering Lectio I may already have something in mind that I refer to as "the other," who can be anyone besides myself. The other may also suddenly become apparent within Lectio. You will also find sometimes if a passage is used more than once in a year or in other years, there are only slight variations in what I write. This is because I believe during these repeated meditations my thoughts, inspirations, perceptions, or concepts become further substantiated.

As you read these short daily Lectio scripture reflections, you will find they have a broad range from the very personal to sometimes external unknown people or situations. My initial Lectio meditative words, phrases or perception are in italics next to the Gospel passage, followed by a brief reflection. My hope is by sharing these vignettes that you will consider exploring your own relationship with God and "the other" through prayer.

May Christ Peace be with you for eternity!

DECEMBER 2019

Sunday, December 1

Matthew 24:37-44 ~ Halfway to Heaven

Have you felt the spiritual touch of the risen Christ, possibly even knowing the physical contact of the divine? Do you believe in the Real Presence of Jesus? Among everything else, doing so allows us in awe to read in the Word about the coming, life and glory of Jesus in the books of the Old Testament. Daily, others are awake when we are not, all over the world praying The Hours (Psalms) which are read or sung with and for us, bringing us halfway to Heaven.

Monday, December 2

Matthew 8:5-11 ~ Become the Centurion

As a Roman Catholic in the U.S. you are familiar with the short prayer said just before communion: "Lord, I am not worthy that you should enter under my roof, but only say the word and my soul shall be healed." When we become the Centurion, our souls become worthy and eternal because we believe the Lord does say the word. Imagine, our awesome Lord, from the distance of less than a breath away, with all the request of the cosmos to consider, responds.

Tuesday, December 3

Luke 10:21-24 ~ Reveal the Father

It is indeed possible with our senses to hear and see that the Father is visible by witnessing the trail of Grace and goodness God leaves in the movement of time. To have Trinity revealed directly is also possible but this movement is not ordinarily experienced through the senses. When the Holy Spirit blesses our soul with an interior awareness of Jesus becoming present to us, we can truly believe that Jesus may have, or will reveal the Father.

Wednesday, December 4

Matthew 15:29-37 ~ Satiate your Spiritual Hunger

Imagine yourself near the Sea of Galilee, the lowest freshwater lake on Earth. You are at the base of the mountain where Jesus is elevated high enough for everyone to see. You watch the procession of those whose faith in Jesus heals them. You have been there three days and despite your hunger you stay, mesmerized by Jesus continuing to give of himself. Then, an even greater miracle occurs; you are fed a tiny piece of food that will both fill you and satiate your spiritual hunger.

Thursday, December 5
Matthew *7:21, 24-27 ~ Knowing God's Will*
Think back to when you first agreed to do God's will. From an early age, I began considering the mystery of knowing God's will but remained lukewarm until a brush with death started a long conversation with God that moved me closer to Mary's Yes. Like many others, a personal experience with 9/11 triggered my own final Yes and I have not looked back. The rain has fallen, floods have come, the winds have blown and buffeted my house, but I am on solid rock, God's will continues to have primacy.

Friday, December 6
Matthew 9:27-31 ~ Fruit of our Being
Like these blind men, Jesus has also actively participated in my life. While I share that Jesus is very much part of my life, I keep the details of the why, how, when and why to myself. My personal thoughts are that I must be like Jesus going to a private "place" to pray, fast, or suffer in secret. If we resist the urge to fully explain our encounters with Jesus, roots us firmly in humility, obedience, and dependence so we can instead focus on revealing the fruit of our being and doing God's will.

Saturday, December 7
Matthew *9:35 – 10:1,5a, 6-8 ~ Can We be Even More*
In my attempt to live an integrated faith life, I cannot help but notice that in every facet of life, especially in work environments, there are many who seem spiritually lost. As Christians we are moved to do something about it. We can be a laborer by being and doing Jesus's truth of helping others feel at ease with being lost, with our compassion, mercy, peace and love, along with sharing what we know of our living Gospel. Can we be even more by following Jesus's will?

Sunday, December 8
Matthew *3:1-12 ~ Voice from the Desert*

Have you ever heard the cry of a voice from the desert? It can be startling and beautiful at the same time. To respond as if it the only thing we have left to do is not easy because the depth of obligations that goes with it slowly gets revealed. As we learn to accept what is asked of us, God will make our path straight. Then at the right time we will be prepared for the metaphor of the winnowing fork throwing the wheat into the air to separate out the grain from the chaff.

Monday, December 9

Luke 1:26-38 ~ Nothing is Impossible with God

When we receive Eucharist, consume the Word or give of ourselves to others, our spiritual wombs fill with refreshing living water. While we are far from Mary's greatness, we can sense our "Yes" helping to wash away the taste of the bitterness of our own imperfections. We learn how Jesus patches over our brokenness by sharing himself with us. We are a humble witness to the received Grace within that outwardly manifest into miracles, as nothing is impossible with God.

Tuesday, December 10

Matthew *18:12-14 ~ Let Jesus Find You*

The parable of the lost sheep seems reversed in today's reality, as the ninety-nine seem lost to worldliness not the one. It is virtually impossible not to desire the same as these ninety-nine. Our senses are being bombarded with how wonderful having everything you want is. Our loving Father's desire is that like a child we are willing turn to Jesus with our "here I am Lord" and let Jesus find you so that we can all rejoice.

Wednesday, December 11

Matthew 11:28-30 ~ Make Our Burdens Light

It would not be appropriate to ask Jesus to carry the weight of all our problems. For instance, we cannot expect difficulties at our jobs to be miraculously resolved, as clearly, most belong to us. Instead, I believe Jesus speaks of the many flavors of evil that surround, tempt, distract, and push us down spiritually. We must strive to completely trust that Jesus's embrace will hold these at bay so we can rest in his love and peace to make our burdens light.

Thursday, December 12

Matthew 2:1-12 ~ Love and being Present

Traditionally when you are invited to a housewarming you seek out the hosts to thank them for their hospitality and give them a gift. The magi knowing the signs and prophecy did the same, as they believed they would meet the new shepherd of the people Israel. Like the Magi, your love and being present to the hosts and all those who are in the dwelling with you is more important than gifts you may have brought. By doing so they will know the place in your heart where Jesus lives.

Friday, December 13

Matthew 11:16-19 ~ Make Room for Jesus

Can you hear the heavenly music playing, calling out to you to dance or mourn? Can you hear John shouting out to make room for Jesus in your heart? Can you eat and drink modesty to proclaim in word, action, prayer and humble presence with the poor or those rich that Jesus loves them? No matter who we might have been we can be made whole if we participate with the Lord who remains dwelling within and among us.

Saturday, December 14

Matthew 17:9a,10-13 ~ Recognize Your Gifts

I know people that can easily recognize someone from their distant past. I cannot, but from personal and witnessed experiences, I know God often elevates other related attributes. For example, I can often sense an inner turmoil in others. This was one of the reasons I discerned I needed to pursue a pastoral ministry education. We are each Elijah and John the Baptist, God wants you to recognize Jesus and your gifts to help restore all things.

Sunday, December 15

Matthew 11:2-11 ~ Walk Towards the Good News

Do you know people whose faith is shaken like the reed being blown this way then that by the wind? If so then this passage is speaking directly to you. With Jesus inside you, you can give them sight, raise their hopes and help them walk towards the Good News. You have already heard John, he has prepared a way for you. You are at minimum the least of the Kingdom of Heaven and greater than John. Jesus is speaking forward in time to you.

Monday, December 16

Matthew 21:23-27 ~ Announce the Coming of Jesus

Zechariah was one of 7000 priest who for the first time in life has a turn to be in the temple. There alone, Gabriel tells him he was to conceive, and his son John was going to announce the coming of Jesus. Over the last thirty years Elizabeth as daughter of a priest and Zechariah must have "witnessed" their son John's mission. How can Herod's corrupt chief priest who feared John prophecy, not answer John's baptism was divine; can we?

Tuesday, December 17
Matthew 1:1-17 ~ Sons and Daughters of God
Matthew 's first words trace Jesus's generations several millennia back to Abraham. I think the effect of doing so grounds the human concept of historical roots and the spiritual reality that we are sons and daughters of God. Many years ago, my father's side of the family mapped our genealogy to the first relative coming to America, back to the early 1600's. It seems to me that they too wanted to feel a beginning in the arms of the Alpha and Omega where history, time, and space merge.

Wednesday, December 18
Matthew 1:18-25 ~ A Special Kind of Love
There are many out there who have not had a father for many reasons. Joseph was on his way to doing one of the normal human reaction of abandonment. It took an angel of the Lord to calm Joseph's fear and treat Jesus as his son. To be a father of a child that is not yours takes a special kind of love, one like Joseph that is filled with righteousness and the grace and love of the Lord.

Thursday, December 19
Luke 1:5-25 ~ Light Within the Darkness
As two holy people, Zechariah and Elizabeth intensely practiced their faith, yet a child did not seem to be part of their plan. They never stopped praying and being righteous. Unexpectedly, divinity answered and as often happens in the interior life, Zechariah entered a significant darkness. Unknown to Zechariah, a wondrous light within the darkness prepared him to raise a humble child filled with the Holy Spirit. St. John the Baptist continues to prepare the way for each of us.

Friday, December 20
Luke 1:26-38 ~ Nothing is Impossible with God
When we receive Eucharist, consume the Word or give of ourselves to others,

our spiritual wombs fill with refreshing living water. While we are far from Mary's greatness, we can sense our "Yes" helping to wash away the taste of the bitterness of our own imperfections. We learn how Jesus patches over our brokenness by sharing himself with us. We are a humble witness to the received Grace within that outwardly manifest into miracles, as nothing is impossible with God.

Saturday, December 21
Luke 1:39-45 ~ To be Blessed
My heart has leap for joy at the expectation of childbirth, receiving Eucharist and in the encounter of a faith filled Christian. The Holy Spirit's prompting creates an invitation to talk, become brother or sister, pray together, help recognize Christ in each other, and add strength to strength. This offer of Mary and Elizabeth to each other, to be blessed and to bless God, is the fruit possible from our unique spiritual wombs.

Sunday, December 22
Matthew 1:18-24 ~ Filled with Righteousness
Most of us would agree that Joseph's reaction of dismissing Mary is justifiable. Imagine how powerful his mystical experience must have been to calm Joseph's fear and treat Jesus as both his and God's son. Like Joseph, if you are a loving father of a child that is not yours I am (we all are) personally grateful as you must be filled with righteousness, grace and trust of the Lord. My prayers today are for the many children out there who do not know their father.

Monday, December 23
Luke 1:57-66 ~ The Hand of the Lord
It is difficult to appreciate the depth of what Elizabeth and Zechariah witnessed, but if you are a parent, you know the blessings of a child. Circumstance played a significant part in spiritually naming one of my children. I felt truly blessed when each of my children was born. I was reminded again at their Baptism and many other times in their life. I am constantly amazed as I observe the hand of the Lord helping with each child as they bring unique beauty into the world.

Tuesday, December 24
Luke 1:67-79 ~ Our Advocate, the Holy Spirit

While we may not be as eloquent as Zechariah, we can still to express how wonderful God is. We hear about the Holy Spirit in scripture prior to Jesus appearance in the upper room through the prophets and holy and righteous people. Our advocate, the Holy Spirit prompts and gives voice to each of our own personally directed prophecies. Let the love, guidance and fruitfulness of the Holy Spirit ring out in your being and with your actions in your own canticle.

Wednesday, December 25
John 1:1-18 ~ Grace Builds Upon Grace
John asks us to believe that Jesus has enlightened us in the Word since the beginning of time and now through His incarnation as one who dwelt among us, fully human and fully divine. If we do, darkness cannot exist, truths are revealed, we cannot be manipulated by the world, grace builds upon grace, and since we are children of God, we will feel inclined to care for and love others. Faith and these reasons among others should compel us to believe.

December 26, Thursday
Matthew 10:17-22 ~ Let the Spirit Speak
When distractions such as negative emotions arrive, my own opinion oftentimes shows rather than allowing the Holy Spirit to speak. I have noticed that the truth of the situation does not come out clear and my insufficient words offer no help for the person or people I am with. Identifying and becoming aware of my weaknesses is slowly allowing me to tamp them down to let the Spirit speak. Belief in the Trinity means we must be present for others even in the worst of our own times.

Friday, December 27
John 20:1a and 2-8 ~ We Know the Risen Lord
If you have lost a loved one, it is likely you have experienced that person's spiritual existence for brief moments throughout your life. You might perceive a gentle touch, vivid thoughts or memories that reassure you that person is with God in Heaven. If we allow it, these moments of not holding on to the physical past can strengthen our beliefs of eternal life and Divinity. Like Mary Magdalen, Simon Peter and disciple Jesus loved, we can say we know the risen Lord.

Saturday, December 28

Matthew 2:13-18 ~ Help Finding Peace
People have been killed throughout history because they do not meet a certain qualification to a certain person or worse a group. Evil that subtlety supports anger and continues to infiltrate our human sphere creates these unjustifiable acts. Due to my father's exposure and one of my children's education, the sadness of the Holocaust is never far from my thoughts. For help finding peace I have learned to weep and pray deeply with Saint Joseph.

Sunday, December 29
Matthew 2:13-15, 19-23 ~ Weep and Pray Deeply with Joseph
No doubt, evil continues to infiltrate the human sphere creating unjustifiable fear and death. Through my father's contribution and one of my children college experience and work, the sadness of the Holocaust never leaves me. It is one of the reasons I have learned to weep and pray deeply with Joseph, so I may counter anger with peace. To be as Joseph means that sometimes we must purposely stay away from "places" where we know evil may be and instead associate with likeminded people.

Monday, December 30
Luke 2:36-40 ~ Worship and Praise God
For most of her years Anna lived what would now be considered a cloistered monastic life of fasting and prayer. If you have visited a monastery or better yet had a retreat at one you can sense the dedication of the men and woman living there. Like Anna they ritually worship and praise God for mercy, compassion, and for favors on us and that we grow to become strong and wise like the child Christ did. In this season of waiting perhaps you could take a minute and bless them for what they do.

Tuesday, December 31
John 1:1-18 ~ Grace Builds Upon Grace
John asks us to believe that Jesus has enlightened us in the Word since the beginning of time and now through His incarnation as one who dwelt among us, fully human and fully divine. If we do, darkness cannot exist, truths are revealed, we cannot be manipulated by the world, grace builds upon grace, and since we are children of God, we will feel inclined to care for and love others. Faith and these reasons among others should compel us to believe.

JANUARY 2020

January 1, Wednesday
Luke 2:16-21 ~ Amazing Words from Others
Have you been like those shepherds leaving their animals unprotected or Mary when God has asked you to step outside your comfort zone? How often have you gone straight to see the newborn Emmanuel; God among us. If you have, are you not evangelizing like the shepherds did? Isn't it a reassuring treasure when the beautiful words spoken to Mary by the shepherds and held in her heart about Jesus resonant for you? Have you heard amazing words from others?

January 2, Thursday
John 1:19-28 ~ Divinities Subtle Whispers
We start our days in our own little deserts where the way begins straight. We hear John the Baptist and others reminding us to walk as the Lord might. To do so is less obvious in the balance of the day as divinities subtle whispers within the cacophony of family friends and work obligations can get in the way. We should not dwell on unworthiness but instead cry out to God for help in allowing the light of Christ inside into the night of the day.

January 3, Friday
John 1:29-34 ~ Baptized with the Holy Spirit
When I enter a church and bless myself with Holy Water from the font with the sign of the Cross, I visualize that I am there with John the Baptist and Jesus in the River Jordan. I see John as a gifted and amazing prophet with unrivaled insights into a realization of who Jesus was to be. John gracefully bows to deeply humble himself as one who baptizes only with cleansing water. He is standing next to Jesus who reminds me that I have been Baptized with the Holy Spirit.

January 4, Saturday
John 1:35-42 ~ Treasured Moments with Jesus
Are you being transformed from one degree of faith to another degree suddenly or gradually? Andrew and Peter followed John the Baptist because

he knew the Messiah was coming. Their rapid moving toward Jesus gave us a deeper appreciation of God's plan for our own transformation. Discipleship occasionally occurs quickly but for most of us very slowly over decades. Within your own journey, I am sure you have treasured moments with Jesus.

Sunday, January 5
Matthew 2:1-12 ~ Love and being Present
Traditionally when you are invited to a housewarming you seek out the hosts to thank them for their hospitality and give them a gift. The magi knowing the signs and prophecy did the same, as they believed they would meet the new shepherd of the people Israel. Like the Magi, your love and being present to the hosts and all those who are in the dwelling with you is more important than gifts you may have brought. By doing so they will know the place in your heart where Jesus lives.

January 6, Monday
Matthew 4:12-17, 23-25 ~ Pray for Yourself
Do wonder interiorly if in your words and actions you are correctly teaching and proclaiming what you believe? Is the spiritual healing in Jesus's name worth the spiritual battle you might be enduring? Is Jesus's light within overshadowing the darkness that surrounds any Christian? If you are withdrawing every day to pray for yourself that you are filled with peace, hope, joy, love of yourself and others then the answer to these questions is yes.

January 7, Tuesday
Mark 6:34-44 ~ How Many Loaves Can I Share
A question for most Christians or those considering practicing their Christianity is how many loaves can I share with others? Mark 6:34-44 is perhaps one of the most striking examples of Jesus's compassion, offering himself to others, and showing us how to love. Can we allow God's love to overfill us so we can do the same? God's grace makes the impossible becomes possible. The same grace that produced food for the crowds is available for the asking.

January 8, Wednesday
Mark 6:45-52 ~ Vigilance in Prayer for Understanding
When personal miracles happen, time seems to soften the experience. We

believed deeply in that moment then we become pulled away. When you get a chance, recall one of these moments. You will likely find it takes great effort to get to the details. Human intellect, worldliness, and the forces that are not God tend to harden our hearts. This is why our relationship with God requires consistent and constant vigilance in prayer for understanding.

January 9, Thursday

Luke 4:14-22 ~ *The Spirit of the Lord*

If we allow ourselves to be filled with the power of the Spirit, we have the ability to show the amazing being present and action of God to those who are spiritually and/or physically in need. Despite all that is around us, we can be a glad sighted person that demonstrates in prayer, word, and actions positive results because the Spirit of the Lord is upon us. To fully accept God's grace means we reflect the love we receive outward to others without hesitation.

January 10, Friday

Luke 5:12-16 ~ *Become the Leper*

I go through several phases when I think it is time to go to confession. First I recall the intensity of the moments that I sinned. I then have to decide if I have already asked for and received forgiveness, especially for those sins that are more minor in nature. As my mind assembles those that are worthy of presenting to the Lord I feel shame. I become the leper, knowing I must prostrate and plead before the Lord to make me clean.

January 13, Monday

Mark 1:14-20 ~ Leaving Self Behind

Although I distinctly remember each of calls from Jesus since youth, it is only in the last decade or so that I have truly understood. As a person of reason and logic, it is often difficult to believe, trust, and discern. Most of the time, my other interest took precedence. The first four decades of my life resulted in only a warm response to these continued invitations. Alone and deep in the forest with a shouting "Yes Lord," I finally I accepted. Have you considered leaving self behind to say "Yes?"

January 14, Tuesday

Mark 1:21-28 ~ The Authority of Jesus Inside

This scripture passage has countlessly let me bring Jesus's response to top of mind when something someone did was bothering me, I was angry, or agitated for no reason. When I am strong in my faith, Jesus helps me to boldly rebuke the forces that do not want me to be calm, at peace or to love. I have had tough times when my faith alone is not enough to create silence, so I must seek out a person who I believe has the authority of Jesus inside.

January 15, Wednesday
Mark 1:29-39 ~ Interrupting Jesus
Can you imagine knowing Jesus personally and interrupting him while he is resting and praying? Yet, this is exactly what Jesus wants from us. If this was not the case, Trinity would not be resident inside us as we are God's tabernacle. God is available to us not just when we or others need healing or chasing away demons but even for the little things, especially those that might lead us to sin. I am constantly challenging myself to know that interrupting Jesus is ok.

January 16, Thursday
Mark 1:40-45 ~ Jesus's Light Inside
Aren't we all a leper in some way? I have several birth defects that I feel make me less of a human. Despite these issues, I believe Jesus has touched me because I approached him. In my journey, to be fully clean in Mary and Joseph's tradition, I offered myself as one of Moses's Israelite's having gone through that prescribed procedure. In belief, even when Jesus is far away, we have the responsibility to allow faith alone to remind us that Jesus's light inside will still be revealed to others.

January 17, Friday
Mark 2:1-12 ~ Rise Through Forgiveness
When Jesus feels we are ready, wrongs that we previously denied or were not aware of are revealed. We have to further process what they are, feel remorse, pray, verbalize them, resolve to not to repeat them, go to Confession if necessary and then be grateful. No doubt saying "Yes" to the purgatory aspects of an interior life is difficult and sometimes we must try as hard as the paralytic man. We fall down, then rise through forgiveness to pick up our mats numerous times in ours live.

January 18, Saturday
Mark 2:13-17 ~ A Movement of the Heart
Jesus calls out to everyone. Scripture passages where Jesus reaches out to

those who are considered sinners or rich by any modern standards are critical moments of God's love. For a modern-day perspective regarding the top 1% wealthiest, consider looking at the Giving Pledge. Almost 150 Billionaires are committed to using the majority of their wealth for Philanthropy. While far from perfect, isn't this at least a movement of the heart in the right direction?

January 19, Sunday
John 1:29-34 ~ Baptized with the Holy Spirit
When I enter a church and bless myself with Holy Water from the font with the sign of the Cross, I visualize that I am there with John the Baptist and Jesus in the River Jordan. I see John as a gifted and amazing prophet with unrivaled insights into a realization of who Jesus was to be. John gracefully bows to deeply humble himself as one who baptizes only with cleansing water. He is standing next to Jesus who reminds me that I have been Baptized with the Holy Spirit.

January 20, Monday
Mark 2:18-22 ~ Adorned Beyond Ordinary Love
I have my favorite pair of jeans, they are a little loose fitting, stained in a few spots, visibly worn thin and reserved for laborious chores. If I am alone with Jesus, I believe these jeans are fine as my thoughts and mind is adorned with love. However, if I am in gathering in any form of community including church or work, I feel my body, mind, and soul must be adorned beyond ordinary love, so I am ready and fresh as I know I am to be or do for the other with God.

January 21, Tuesday
Mark 2:23-28 ~ See as God Sees
In today's scripture, Jesus allows us to see as God sees; straight into the hardened hearts of men, like David who knew the breadth and depth of God's love. There can be no doubt that with our own anointing as future "David's," means we must prioritize mercy and compassion for our neighbor. This truth of Jesus, asking us to paint well outside of the lines we are comfortable with, should be even more obvious on Sabbath when Christ is at the top of our heart and mind.

January 22, Wednesday

Mark 3:1-6 ~ Restoring Luster to The Garden
During the growing season, my wife and I along with a number of other people gather after Mass on Sunday to work at the church's community garden. Produce from the garden goes to the local food pantry. It is our way of stretching out our hands to make a stranger's life a little easier. It is more than that as in my heart I know our little effort is restoring luster to "The Garden" on the same Sabbath day that Jesus did.

January 23, Thursday
Mark 3:7-12 ~ Love Refills our Emptiness
Jesus understands the limits of our humanity. For example, when we remember our yesterdays, many of those days were filled with uplifting glory. However, we are in the world with challenging days when we must withdraw in prayer to wait while God's calming sustenance and love refills our emptiness. Trinity's giving of joy and peace then helps us to reject the weight surrounding us so like Jesus we can be available for others.

January 24, Friday
Mark 3:13-19 ~ Christ has Called You
Has Jesus summoned you? Have you turned towards him in conversation? Perhaps as you walk with Jesus, you have certainty that He is walking with you. In faith, do you believe in the gift of His authority within you? Consider that after the Apostles moment of summoning you have two millennia more history. If you have not already, push aside any doubts that in this moment our Glorified Christ has called you to be and do with Him.

January 25, Saturday
Mark 16:15-18 ~ Our Shared Journey
I have to keep reminding myself that there is an order to what Jesus ask of us. Believe, be baptized, and then go into the world to proclaim the Word. In our continuing belief, if we use Jesus's name in faith and love there will be signs. However, these signs are not the goal. Instead, in profound humility we need to work with Jesus as the world desperately needs saving and to know Jesus's embrace. We must be witnesses in our shared journey as a drop in a vast ocean of drops.

January 26, Sunday
Matthew 4:12-23 ~ Answer Jesus with a Yes

Have you wondered if in words and actions you are teaching and proclaiming like Jesus's first disciple? Is the spiritual healing you are doing in Jesus's name worth the battles like John the Baptist you might be enduring? Is Jesus's light within overshadowing the darkness in the world that surrounds you? Do not forget to withdraw every day to pray, filling yourself with peace, hope, joy, love so that you answer Jesus with a yes.

January 27, Monday

Mark 3:22-30 ~ Cast Aside our Divisions

As Christians, we are believers in the love between Jesus and the Father that we know as the Holy Spirit. Yet, throughout our history, the sly fox of the other side has been and continues to disrupt our ability to unite in the Trinity's principles of not just love but mercy and compassion. It is time we cast aside divisions in order that we might fully receive and reflect this glorious light. Our responsibility is to help those who newly enter God's sphere recognize eternal life.

January 28, Tuesday

Mark 3:31-35 ~ Joining Christ in Community

I used to think that my family consisted of my wife and children, a brother and sisters, other relatives as well as all my in-laws. Then I began to understand that my family further rippled out to church friends, colleagues, and those I knew in heaven. Now, interiorly I am aware that I must extend beyond this circle, joining Christ in community, unconditionally offering myself as needed to all brothers and sisters, sharing His sacrifice, peace, food, and love.

January 29, Wednesday

Mark 4:1-20 ~ Our Trail of Fruit

For a moment recall the last time that you thought about the beliefs in the Creed or Lord's Prayer as you recited them? Strongly put, Christ in stories, parables and metaphors is asking us to believe and understand the Word, not to just recite it. To do so is not easy because the deeper our belief, the more difficult tribulations, distractions and temptations become. In fact, they are among the signs of true belief along our path but just as important is our trail of fruit.

January 30, Thursday

Mark 4:21-25 ~ Trinity's Gifts will Increase
When we know Jesus is directly calling us, we say, "Yes Lord, your servant is listening." Other times we are surprised when we suddenly realize we have been called repeatedly. It is not easy to discern and understands calls that are more subtle. It may be because the other side has been tempting our ego, we may not feel qualified, or it feels like our light is already burning bright enough. In our stillness, if we truly know and accept that more can being measured out, Trinity's gifts will increase.

January 31, Friday
Mark 4:26-34 ~ Beautiful Blossoming Seeds
Jesus as the living Word describes our maturing into the kingdom of God in a variety of parables regarding seeds. God "plants" Grace within us with the full knowledge of the expected effect. We do not need to know the precise plan for Grace, but simply trust that either our needs or the needs of our neighbor will be involved. Our free will "Yes" allows Grace to interiorly nurture us into beautiful blossoming seeds so that while on earth, God can become visible to others.

FEBRUARY 2020

February 1, Saturday

Mark 4:35-41 ~ Discovering Weakness Without Jesus

I have been tossed about in wave after wave of discomfort(s). I have forgotten that Jesus is just a thought away. I know that the Holy Spirit's gift of courage is in every breath, yet I had to be reminded that unceasing prayer is necessary to melt distractions away. Sometimes our faith becomes as thin as a spiders strand in these worst of times, wavering in the wind, but not lost. In our own defense, the disciples who could touch Jesus, spent time discovering weakness without Jesus.

February 2, Sunday

Luke 2:22-40 ~ Praise and Bless You God

Years ago fresh off a Hebrew Scriptures course, I noticed the frequency of blessing and praising God in the Old Testament. Abraham blessed and praised God for his sons. The Psalms consistently sing of blessing and praising God. Without missing a Scriptural heartbeat, through Luke's eyes we encounter Anna and Simeon who blesses and praises God, Mary, and Joseph. It is our turn; praise and bless you God for all old and new encounters with us.

February 3, Monday

Mark 5:1-20 ~ Trust What Jesus has Done for You

Jesus's dramatic response of mercy even with evil spirits shows us the true meaning of the power of authority. For example, in your response to gossip, do you join in, remain silent, or try to change the conversation? I know from experience that if you trust what Jesus has done for you, you will often find you can change the conversation. While not as dramatic as Legion in scripture, your small effort can give you a sense of how much more is possible.

February 4, Tuesday

Mark 5:21-43 ~ Little Girl, Arise

I find it interesting that Bible tradition has Jesus speaking the Aramaic

"Talitha koum" despite whatever the translation might be. As a child of God, I am sure you have heard Jesus speak the words "little girl, arise" to you. Even with life's numerous confrontations, our challenge is to awake more fully, rising in faith to all. Faith with Grace reduces fear, opens our hearts, creates empathy, and wraps us in the cloak of Christ so we may touch and embrace conditions such as suffering by "the other".

February 5, Wednesday
Mark 6:1-6 ~ The Impossible becomes Possible
I am broken and weak in many ways, yet with prayer, faith, and trust in Jesus, these deficiencies are temporarily repaired as needed. I am especially aware of this when I am in a ministry situation. There is often a pause when I share one of these mini-miracles with someone for the first time. Their expressive smile lets me know if their own faith believes that this is possible. It is a beautiful cycle as my own faith is also strengthened because the belief in receiving unveils that the impossible becomes possible.

February 6, Thursday
Mark 6:7-13 ~ Put our Gifts to Use
Christ's instructional metaphors apply to our own journeys. To take nothing at minimum means leaving behind certain thoughts (and objects) to which we are attached. It is not easy, as most of us have long list of these attachments that take many years to remove. Some are extremely difficult to put aside. I believe God wants us to start our unique ministry efforts even before we are purified because much is revealed along the way. God's only expectation is that we will put our gifts to use.

February 7, Friday
Mark 6:14-29 ~ Cry Out for God's Mercy
The same evil that rippled through the generations of Biblical "Herod's" continues to modern times, influencing the desire for some to have total domination. Throughout the world, innocents fear for their lives. It is a complex moral issue because the answer is not always fighting fire with fire. We are not without hope as our Christian obligation is to cry out for God's mercy. As a crowd of two or more, in memory of John the Baptist, Peter and others, in Jesus's name we pray; "Satan get behind us".

February 8, Saturday

Mark 6:30-34 ~ The Gift of a Deserted Place
I have an early morning routine where I am able to pray and rest in silence. I am extremely grateful for this, as I know it is not practical for many. If you know the gift of a "deserted place", you are likely aware that it comes with the responsibility of reflecting the gathered light. With great joy and humility, the basket cover comes off to share and teach of the wondrous love of Jesus whether internally, a moment the Spirit presents to you, or in a planned ministry.

February 9, Sunday

Matthew 5:13-16 ~ Christ's Light
To be humble is to be modest with our own importance, not showy, and unassuming. How is it then possible to be an unhidden light, shining bright enough for everyone to see? Ah… it is gloriously doable if the light that is showing is Christ's light not our own. Jesus teaches us that people will see this light much easier if we are not boastful or hypocritical. This light is a quiet "being and doing" for God and others without expecting anything in return.

February 10, Monday

Mark 6:53-56 ~ Touch Jesus's Cloak
Many adult years passed until I began to deeply believe Trinity lived within, influencing everything I am if I allow it. In all honestly, I knew the call since youth, but I was not ready. When I finally asked to touch Jesus's cloak, a holistic healing began, some of which I cannot properly describe. One certainty rose to the surface; I had to be present to others. I have lost track of the number of times that I know Jesus inside me has positively affected someone else.

February 11, Tuesday

Mark 7:1-13 ~ Let God's Love Surface
Through an endless list of products and services, society portrays that we must be clean and perfect externally. Shouldn't it be that we are pure inside is what really matters? We are challenged to let our vices manifest but can that choice always be blamed on outside influences? The hidden truth is that we must be willing to depend and reach out to the holiness of Jesus when desires flare up, re-directing thoughts towards our heart to let God's love surface.

February 12, Wednesday

Mark 7:14-23 ~ Evil Intentions

We are heavily influenced by more than just unclean food. In society today, it seems like everything is ok to do or say anything creating the singular "I" and we can become the judge of right and wrong. Doesn't this distorted moral compass and the hidden nature of evil intentions make it possible to ignore our neighbor? To place oneself as the center, is the personal defilement that Jesus speaks of, because both God and neighbor become less discernible.

February 13, Thursday

Mark 7:24-30 ~ Honest Compassion

How many times in your life have you changed your opinion after carefully listening to the opposing view? Isn't that what Jesus himself does with the Syrophoenician woman? She was not of the same culture as Jesus and his initial human reaction was to effectively ignore her. However, her argument touched His heart causing Him to re-consider the situation and truly pay attention to her needs. Does this painful story of honest compassion touch a nerve for you?

February 14, Friday

Mark 7:31-37 ~ Astounded Beyond Measure

A decade ago, when I put my hearing aids on for the first time, sounds that I had never heard before overwhelmed me with tears of joy. One of the most beautiful was the music of evening tree frogs. Years earlier, after deep prayer another disability began being offset by Jesus's compassion, allowing me to read out loud without jumbling words for the first time. No doubt like the crowd, when appropriate, I tell the stories of how I have been astounded beyond measure after I said Yes to the Lord.

February 15, Saturday

Mark 8:1-10 ~ Jesus as Spiritual Food

In Jesus's role as a teacher, He knows that in order to share like He does, the disciples must first know how to satisfy basic human needs. Otherwise, they could not understand spiritual needs. Jesus desires the same for us. We must be able to approach those who need bodily food, and equally as well with those who are over satisfied in luxuries. Our offer is to share what we have within ourselves; Jesus as spiritual food. Like Jesus, our spiritual mercy and compassion cannot be conditional.

February 16, Sunday
Matthew 5:17-37~ Help Others in Their Journey
We must carefully interpret the law that God breathed into the Old Testament
and not include what man has created outside of the Spirits inspiration. Jesus
helps define these better throughout the Gospels, always pointing back to the
love of God and neighbor. As Christians, we learn and teach by example to
respect, forgive, have compassion, mercy, peace and project the spiritual
ways of love if we are to find and help others in their journey towards
Heaven.

February 17, Monday
Mark 8:11-13 ~ Magnificent Signs of Heaven
For many, signs from Heaven are miraculous physical phenomena that can be
recognized by sense. I believe these are mainly consolations for those that
need a little boost of faith. The most significant signs from Heaven manifest
from deep within the heart without conditions. These gifts allow grace to
overpower evil, bring peace, and mirror Jesus. They result in the fruit of faith
that just knows, hope, love, mercy, and compassion. How can these not be
magnificent signs of Heaven?

February 18, Tuesday
Mark 8:14-21~ Count on Jesus
I am certain that you have had times in your life that you had a desperate
situation, but you were comforted before it got overwhelming. Jesus teaches
us that if we trust Him, then we will be at peace. Yet, it seems like the cycle
is new each time, as we tend to forget that we have to look towards Jesus.
Sometimes, only when we begin to get emotional do we remember to pray
and reach out for help. We know the solution, but if you are like me, the
struggle to count on Jesus has lasted for my entire life.

February 19, Wednesday
Mark 8:22-26 ~ Jesus's love and Eucharist
Yes ago, before a personal schedule change, I was able to bring Eucharist and
conversation to the homes of the sick. In this decade long period, I witnessed
miracles of healing of both the physical and the heart. The most significant
were those who knew death was a short-term reality for them. Their belief in
God increased, they were able to begin to see Heaven as beauty and splendor
prior to their passing. They understood Jesus's love and Eucharist let them do

so clearly.

February 20, Thursday
Mark 8:27-33 ~ Set our Mind on Divine Things
Shouldn't we be asking the question "Who do people say that I am?" of ourselves? If we could listen in on conversations of our friends and family, would we hear them saying that we are a Christian because they know we go to Church? Deeper yet, would we hear them discussing our prayer life or what we do for others. Would they question why we deny our own suffering and needs to do so? Would they understand why we turn from evil to instead set our mind on Divine things?

February 21, Friday
Mark 8:34 – 9:1~ Dare to Look into your Heart
If you ever dare to look into your heart to ask Jesus if you are the Christian He wants you to be, you will have to determine if you are suffering in silence in some way. Without knowing significant discomfort, it is nearly impossible to actually be like Jesus. Another related sign is that you are dedicating a major portion of your life to "the other" by loving, praying, being present, or doing. This means that even in your work life you notice these signs.

February 22, Saturday
Matthew 16:13-19 ~ Thank you Peter!
Jesus Christ my savior, has held out his hand to save me from drowning in sorrow, selfishness, anger, pride, greed, and even briefly denying divinities existence, yet, here I am; deeply in love with God. This would not have been possible without the rock of my Church community. When I walk through those metaphorical doors, God is silently waiting to embrace me, rescue me from my sins, nourish me, and to confirm that my humanity actually mingles with divinity. Thank you Peter!

February 23, Sunday
Matthew 5:38-48 ~ Christ's Peace within the Cacophony
In an intense moment of pure evil, I did not react. God's responded with an instant miracle gift reversing a life-long learning disability of writing. Thomas Merton quotes: "If you write for God, you will reach many men and bring them joy. If you write for men, you may make some money and you may give someone a little joy and you may make noise in the world, for a

little while." I write anonymously to witness in a noiseless joy of my ongoing conversion, reflecting on the moments of Christ's peace within the cacophony.

February 24, Monday

Mark 9:14-29 ~ Rejecting Evil Requires Prayer

Many would say that Jesus healed the boy's epilepsy, hearing, and speaking, but believers know that the boy was also under spiritual attack. I have directly witnessed evil operating within otherwise intelligent, healthy people. So why couldn't evil also be present in the boy without the parents' consent? Jesus not only had to heal him physically, he had to force the worst kind of evil out, the kind that is not subtle, but publicly makes itself known. Rejecting the entire range of evil requires prayer and belief.

February 25, Tuesday

Mark 9:30-37 ~ Humbly Serving Children

We have the advantage of knowing what the disciples had yet to comprehend. What remains for us is to welcome the risen Jesus into our entire being. Jesus has taught us that children are important, they deserve to be loved, and we should be ready to do anything for our children. Please join me for a moment to pray for those wish to know Christ better by humbly serving children and all those young and old whose disabilities limit them to childhood needs.

February 26, Wednesday

Matthew 6:1-6,16-18 ~ God is Man's Beautifier

What Jesus speaks of reminds me of a haunting verse from the song Grace; "Grace makes beauty out of ugly things." Among other things, private prayer and fasting exposes the interior unknowns of the ugly things of our heart and mind to consider. Our Father's response to our prayer and secret sacrifices can yield generous wisps of undeserved Grace far beyond our ability to humbly express its joy. For me, this is proof that God is man's beautifier.

February 27, Thursday

Luke 9:22-25 ~ Join Jesus on the Cross

Obviously, we cannot compare our physical and spiritual suffering to Christ as his was for everyone past, present and future. However, the same signs of Jesus's selflessness and the ability to suffer silently are one of the marks of a practicing and maturing Christian. Pastorally, I refer to this passage whenever I encounter someone progressing along the path of following Jesus. I do not soften the fact that Christ is upfront about the commitments required to join Jesus on the Cross.

February 28, Friday
Matthew 9:14-15 ~ Willingly Change
Living the Christian life is filled with inconsistencies. At times we must embrace the known, behaving within whatever constraints, customs and traditions that may exist. Other times we are in unexplored territory where everything is new, and we must be prepared for anything. A Christian's challenge is not to fit our square block into a round hole but to discern then willingly change into the shape God may be asking of us.

February 29, Saturday
Luke 5:27-32 ~ Becoming Transformed
When Jesus dines with the large crowd of tax collectors, He gives them an opportunity to accept forgiveness and love so they may walk this same path. If we have interiorly experienced the misery of moral and spiritual poverty, we too are becoming transformed. When we then encounter situations such excessiveness, worldliness, superiority, or even those who ignore others what are we to do? Without judgment, we must humbly, gently, and willingly offer the joy of our own being cured.

MARCH 2020

March 1, Sunday

Matthew 4:1-11 ~ Trust God without Bargaining

Have you ever tried to make a deal with God; if you give me what I want I will do what you want? Maybe you have tried the same thing with your spouse or even a friend. We are tempted all the time to expect something in return for favors we might do. The Devil promising Jesus everything in return for all Jesus could see, reminds us to instead trust God without bargaining or obligation. Lord, praise you for all you have unconditionally done for us.

March 2, Monday

Matthew 25:31-46 ~ Righteousness

Not all virtues are as clear as righteousness; either you are right, or you are wrong. Either you believe Jesus Christ means we must treat others as we treat ourselves or be selfish. Either we are all one in mind, body and soul or we are not. If we are never hungry, can drink fresh water anytime, have shelter, are clothed and have access to medicine; then we must attempt to bring equality with either our time, talent or treasures to others or we cannot believe we are righteous.

March 3, Tuesday

Matthew 6:7-15 ~ On Earth as it is in Heaven

Years ago, Fr. Joe enlightened me with a discussion of "on earth as it is in heaven." I suggested that there was not a hard line between heaven and earth and to my surprise he agreed. He said that the Father through Christ has made Heaven already "partially" here, but not fully revealed. For a few examples: we can perceive a taste of heaven when we sense God's presence, consume Christ in Eucharist or Word, engage the wonder of the cosmos, and hear the words I love you and then love back.

March 4, Wednesday

Luke 11:29-32 ~ Listening to the Wisdom

You may have asked for a small sign from God. If God was generous, you may have received a feeling that all will be well, peace, warmth from within, or perhaps a sense of increasing faith. Classically, one of the lasting effects of these acknowledgments is the desire to identify and judge interior wrongs. These accumulating moments can result in ongoing multiple conversions. Listening to this wisdom, you can grow in certainty that Christ must be present now, in the past, and into the future.

March 5, Thursday
Matthew 7:7-12 ~ Knocking on our Door
What are your expectations from friends, family, and strangers? Do you want the warmth of their love, isn't trust near the top of your list, what about respect, faith in them, and their dependability? If we are not giving to them beforehand, how can we expect others to help us in our worst of times? The truth is that we need to be grateful that they could be knocking on our door at any time. God stands ready to rain Grace upon Grace upon those who do.

March 6, Friday
Matthew 5:20-26 ~ Resolve Turmoil Quickly
How people behave is often shaped by their circumstance. I try to keep this in mind as I learn to minimize my reaction to an offense. In all honesty, I still have interior frustration even if I limit my outward response. In truth, it is a righteousness test, as improving how I handle myself in these situations does not come easy. I still have to remember to quickly seek Christ's help to resolve turmoil, because I know peace comes, and then I can forgive and forget.

March 7, Saturday
Matthew 5:43-48 ~ Love's Perfection
We are filled with love from the Word, Eucharist and witnessing God's promise to us. We cannot forget that even for those without this heightened awareness, Grace rains down equally. Willingly receiving Trinity's love begins with the responsibility of transcending negatives that come our way. Deeper still, God can break the bonds that hold us back from true wholeness. We are free to believe that Jesus inside, as love's perfection, is there for us to unconditionally give it all away to everyone we encounter.

March 8, Sunday
Matthew 17:1-9 ~ You are God's Beloved

The transfiguration is one of those scenes that that we all seem to have a similar visualization. Was this mystical experience a one-time event, arranged just for Peter, James and John? When you place yourself with them, doesn't the Word come alive; don't you see Jesus in the dazzling light and, hear the Father speaking? Do not be afraid of your own experiences of consolation. You are God's beloved son or daughter, with whom He is well pleased.

March 9, Monday
Luke 6:36-38 ~ Repeating Measures of Grace
In physics, an echo returned greater than it began is an impossibility, but not true with God's grace. The Father's genuine love as mercy is metered out freely without prejudice. We are the echo, responsible for helping Grace reach into places it has never been. We may not be able to end a war, but perhaps the repeating measures of Grace we accept can raise our neighbor's hope, settle an argument, change a sinner's heart, or heal an inner wound.

March 10, Tuesday
Matthew 23:1-12 ~ Cast Christ's Love Outward
I wear hearing aids to help with a humbling hearing loss. The replacement (un)gift is sensitive skin that is always conscious. But, ah... the hidden Rosary around my neck has to only slightly move to remind me that Christ is present wherever I may be. We each live with our own burdens, but unseen Grace lifts us up. Isn't it appropriate that we should not seek false love, but quietly cast Christ's love outward from within?

March 11, Wednesday
Matthew 20:17-28 ~ My Chalice You Will Indeed Drink
"My chalice you will indeed drink." This chalice, overflowing with love also includes suffering. Paraphrasing St. Paul, Jesus is in our body, manifested in our mortal flesh. No doubt, we are God's containers. Our hearts must fill abundantly with the Spirit's, Jesus's and the Father's grace(s), mercy and compassion. As difficult as it seems to believe, to serve as vessels means we must actually participate in the mystery of Christ's death and resurrection in whatever way God gives us.

March 12, Thursday
Luke 16:19-31 ~ Carried Away by Angels

Belief, repentance and helping those less fortunate before being asked, are all woven within Jesus's story of the Rich Man and Lazarus. Jesus is also reminding us that we too get the opportunity to be carried away by angels to be with Abraham. We preview the joy possible when the fullness of Heaven arrives for us beyond physical doing; as we immersive ourselves in the practice "being" by reflecting and being present with Christ's love, praying, and consuming the Word and Eucharist.

March 13, Friday

Matthew 21:33-43, 45-46 ~ Become a Cornerstone

As active Christians we need to occasionally confirm that we see the signs of fruits of the Holy Spirit in our lives. Love, joy, peace, patience and many other stabilizing or growth virtues should be readily apparent. Our faith and beliefs reflecting outward helps to produce additional fruit for the Kingdom, as we are attracting others to be Christ like. Firmly established we can become a cornerstone with Jesus, doing and "being present."

March 14, Saturday

Luke 15:1-3, 11-32 ~ Prodigal Son

Rembrandt's Prodigal Son painting hangs prominently in the most used room of our house. In all honesty, I have been the son, lost and barely going through the motions of being Christian. I have returned multiple times to be embraced by the Father's love. I have also been the jealous son. I am coming up on almost 20 years of dying to "self." I have slowly begun transforming to being father. The constant sting of the other side's taunting and tempting reminds me I must be vigilant, pray, consume, and share Christ.

March 15, Sunday

John 4:5-42~ It is Easy to Become a Disciple

Recall the feelings you had when you really connected with someone talking about Jesus. My most powerful stories are when I allow my emotions to show through about something Jesus did for me. When I am truly focused in the conversation, especially in times of sorry or regret, faith lets me know peace, love and hope is flowing to the other. Like the Woman at the well, when Jesus is integrated into our life it is easy to become a disciple.

March 16, Monday

Luke 4:24-30 ~ Walk Softly

Have you ever stepped into a crowd to discover you were the only person that practiced your faith? It is a surreal situation as immediately your antenna goes up for help from God. Your whole body gets involved as your senses become heightened. Everything depends on how you behave and what you say. Do you forcibly insert God into the conversation, remain silent, or perhaps walk softly recognizing yours and others feelings and emotions?

March 17, Tuesday
Matthew 18:21-35 ~ Softened by Grace
Not so long ago, I knew I had to fall down to my knees more often, forgive where forgiveness seemed unworthy, and embrace when the battle inside said not to. As I began to do so in faith, I have encountered the heart of Jesus, a heart the color of love. In these brief moments, I have been softened by grace to receive the kind of love, peace, and joy that last for eternity. To know true forgiveness, I must allow the confrontations of my own will to be superseded by eternity's light in the darkness.

March 18, Wednesday
Matthew 5:17-19 ~ Breathed into Scripture
The law that God has breathed into Scripture must be carefully interpreted to not include what man creates outside of the Spirits inspiration. Jesus helps us with the critical thoughts of the law throughout the Gospels, which can be summarized in just a few words; Love God and neighbor. We must first love ourselves so we can help others in their journey towards Heaven. We lead by following Christ's example of love by being humble, respectful, forgiving, having compassion, mercy, and peace.

March 19, Thursday
Matthew 1:16, 18-21, 24a ~ From our Beginning to Our End
It has always amazed me to hear this passage to consider Matthews genealogy mapping of Jesus's generations spanning the millennia back to Abraham. This reaching back to our own historical roots grounds us in our human reality. Just as important is the reality that we are sons and daughters of God, and brothers and sisters to Emmanuel with us. Like Joseph, without fear, we can place ourselves spiritually in the arms of the Alpha and Omega, with us from our beginning to our end.

March 20, Friday

Mark 12:28-34 ~ Change Vices into Virtues
To speak and feel against peace in your heart, love, and a sense of belonging to divinity are just some of the injustices with the Holy Spirit that Jesus warns of. Since Baptism, the Spirit has taken up residence within, guiding your journey towards union with God. Through you, the Spirit's gifts can help show others that the Kingdom of God is already arriving. I am a witness that with cooperation, the Holy Spirit can in abundance change vices into virtues.

March 21, Saturday
Luke 18:9-14 ~ Be Merciful to Me
I look forward to the sacred times when I confess my major sins to a Priest and receive forgiveness from God. I personally find it a more difficult to confess more minor sins in my private space of prayer. I must directly ask God to be merciful to me a sinner, if I am to seek deep prayer distant from everything else. If I cannot, then I am not truly righteous or humble. Most of the time, the first attempt fails, because I become aware of the contempt written on my heart and I must work on erasing it.

March 22, Sunday
John 9:1-41~ I was blind but now I see
God does listen to sinners; otherwise, I suspect there would be very little communication between God and anyone in the world. Even with my imperfections, Jesus has helped me to see, be grateful, and use his gifts. I have personally experienced the wondrous effect of being repentant, then extending what I have learned using Jesus's example into others' lives. Have you witnessed the washing and healing ripple of Jesus's love?

March 23, Monday
John 9:1-41 ~ I was blind but now I see
God does listen to sinners; otherwise, I suspect there would be very little communication between God and anyone in the world. Even with my imperfections, Jesus has helped me to see, be grateful, and use his gifts. I have personally experienced the wondrous effect of being repentant, then extending what I have learned using Jesus's example into others' lives. Have you witnessed the washing and healing ripple of Jesus's love?

March 24, Tuesday

John 5:1-16 ~ When We Have Been Made Well

In the ordinary course of accepting Jesus as Savior, there will be obstacles in the way. It holds true especially for continuing to keep Jesus at the top of our mind and actions. These obstacles are surprisingly not being poor, ostracized, or neglected but rather self-desire and evil that subtly weaves into our lives. When we have been made well then accept the invitation to walk with Jesus, our task is to remain pure and sinless otherwise we become part of the worldly crowd.

March 25, Wednesday

Luke 1:26-38 ~ Grace that Manifests into Miracles

Imagine that even if you are a man, you have a spiritual womb. It is your hidden place for divinities love to grow, be present for you, and able to be integrated into your whole self. You are aware that what is in your womb can be given to others. You are filled with refreshing living water that strengthens your weaknesses and fills in your imperfections. You are a humble witness to the gift of Grace that manifests into miracles, as nothing is impossible with God.

March 26, Thursday

John 5:31-47 ~ Witnesses for the Truth

Am I a witness, do I reflect light, and what of my own journey towards the Cross? There are times when I lead the Rosary and my Dysgraphia kicks in, making a Hail Mary becomes unrecognizable. Yet, fellow believer's strong voices know to continue. Sorrow for me is no longer whispered, the Holy Spirit's gift of courage takes over, and bumps smooth out in the mingling. Yes, these are witnesses for the truth; faith's light wins each time, everyone shares Jesus's Glory.

March 27, Friday

John 7:1-2, 10, 25-30 ~ I Know Christ

Challenged, I am going to encounter my world today as an integrated Christian. I think I am doing ok with being righteous, my ethics are intact, and I care about others, all necessary human virtues. But, should I leave divinity within hidden away in secret, or open doors of the Tabernacle that Jesus asks that I should be? With this newfound growing courage, maybe I can start with a whisper, first revealing that I know Christ.

March 28, Saturday

John 7:40-53 ~ Peace not Division

Well over a decade has passed since I participated an unprovoked attack on Catholics and their "Rosaries." The man that did so was shocked when I showed him the Rosary I wear. I asked if he prayed for and with people he knew in heaven. His yes let me question what was wrong with doing so with Mary the mother of Christ. His misplaced anger melted when I shared that the Rosary points me in the direction of Jesus's love for us. I will never forget the smile in agreement that our world needs peace not division.

March 29, Sunday

John 11:1-45 ~ Christ's Tears of Living Water

I have lost track of the times I waited for Jesus to show up, watched him from the crowd, mourned without including him, been angry with him and been selfishly human with him. Despite this, why does he continue to call me out from my cave of comfortable shadows? Perhaps, my own awakening is the realization to believe that whatever darkness maybe around me, Christ's tears of living water brings life to those who are thirsty.

March 30, Monday

John 8:1-11 ~ Within our Heart

Before you get upset at someone else, do you first look within, especially at those times you have done something similar? Like me, if you are honest with yourself, you are probably not looking often enough. I believe by silently writing on the ground, Jesus was giving the scribes and Pharisees time to emphasize an interior examination of their own sins. Isn't Jesus always within our heart to help us with this? Our challenge in loving neighbor is to remember this process of forgiving.

March 31, Tuesday

John 8:21-30 ~ Walking with Jesus in the Above

I vividly remember the first time I truly looked up at a human cast in bronze, mounted on a wooden Cross. At that moment Jesus began to lift me up to places I had not known. Our journeys include a transformational belief in a Jesus Christ who is with us now and even more so after death to self, in an above not of this world. We can continue to transform from belief to actually walking with Jesus in the above, embraced by the loving arms of I Am.

APRIL 2020

April 1, Wednesday

John 8:31-42 ~ Turn Toward the Source

After a formal Reconciliation, if you have felt free from sin and forgiven others, then you know true peace. For a moment, all is right with the world and your heart is filled with love. Having been in Jesus's presence, you can do no harm and are ready to "do what you have heard from the Father." Unfortunately, like a balloon slowly losing air, our newfound freedom slips away but we know Christ is there for us to turn toward the source again for help.

April 2, Thursday

John 8:51-59 ~ Tasting Death

Years ago, after reading this passage I wrote a poem for Jesus titled "Nine Lives", below is the last Stanza:

At fifty I died a different death, a haunting lasting death to self
This pain of recognizing others needs greater than anything felt
At fifty-three it's a daily death, as night time calls each day end
God's peace settles in, refreshing me for tomorrow's resurrection

April 3, Friday

John 10:31-42 ~ God's Sons and Daughters

The claim; we are children of God. Witness to miracles; yes. Love God and neighbor; yes. Good works; yes. Listen to the Word; yes. Community; yes. Believe that Christ inside is our brother; yes. Forgive others; yes. Do we blaspheme; yes – but it is against a disconnected society that is rejecting an integrated faith life. There are metaphoric stones being thrown at us, but the truth of the Cross and Trinity of Father, Son, and Holy Spirit living inside us, guides and protects us.

April 4, Saturday

John 11:45-56 ~ Gathered into One

It seems to me that we should strive to be like each of the Mary's in scripture; Mary the mother of Christ, Mary who anointed Jesus with perfumed oil,

Mary the sister of Martha and Mary the repentant sinner. There is no middle ground as the other option is to be like those who did nothing or worse went to the Pharisees. Our ultimate choice is to participate in receiving and giving unconditional love or living in unending darkness.

April 5, Sunday
Matthew 26:14 – 27:66 ~ Three times
Years ago, in an evening before Palm Sunday I went to bed with the thought of why was Christ born to die? I woke at midnight, disturbed by a pain I could not explain, but my prayer calmed. Later again I sensed pain filled with sorrow, prayer settled me into peace. I rose as dawn entered, in a very dark pain. In prayer that time, I came to understand I must accept my share. Three times, I had asked the Lord to take care of me, three times Christ divine illumed to join with my suffering.

April 6, Monday
Luke 4:16-21 ~ Pass through the Crowd
Jesus is quoting a timeless question from an ancient Jewish Midrash exploring Genesis. How can Jesus, the son of the carpenter Joseph know so much and be able to cure others? They did not understand that Jesus was also God's son. As an active Christian haven't you experienced the same question, if not it is likely you will? As children of God we know the source for all we might do or be for others. Yet, like Jesus, we sometimes have to pass through the crowd because our belief is rejected.

April 7, Tuesday
John 13:21-33. 36-38 ~ Betrayed and Denied Christ
I had a function after Church, I couldn't waste time gabbing. I had grown impatient waiting for multiple light cycles because I was among all the cars leaving the Church parking lot. The bridge construction ahead meant I had to drive even faster. In a glance to my left I felt the feather touch from the Cross on my chest; evil had penetrated, I had betrayed and denied Christ three times in just a few minutes. In my sorrow, I felt unconditional love flow; I knew I had permission to try again.

April 8, Wednesday
Matthew 26:14-25 ~ Surely not I, Lord
As I have gotten to know Jesus through Lent, it seems easy to imagine that an

unknown but certain man says "Yes" when asked to open his home to "strangers" for a meal. His acceptance invites the Passion story to begin. He is witness to an event of epic proportions. From his eyes I see the conversation move off center, Christ's betrayer has dipped his hand into the unnamed man's bowl. The instant when the bowl contained both darkness and light still echoes; surely not I, Rabbi.

April 9, Thursday
John 13:1-15 ~ Wash the Feet in Front of Me
Prayer of Pedilavium:
You kneeled down in front of me to wash my feet
To let me reach into the depth of Your humbleness
This from a man who could have everything
All You want in return is a shadow of Your kindness
Bless me with gifts of Your love for community
Let my tears of gratefulness join in the bowl
So I too, can humbly wash the feet in front of me

April 10, Friday
John 18:1 -- 19:42 ~ Holy Friday
Prayer of Veneratio:
I place myself among the crowd watching You
sadness finds itself penetrating every thought
I so want to shout out, stop no more of this
but I have learned this is the way it must be
As move with the crowd and the way towards You
sadness slowly turns to thankfulness
My turn now to touch and feel loves tenderness
As I walk among the crowd I encounter every day
I must remember, because of You, I am also raised

April 11, Saturday Holy
Matthew 28:1-10 ~ Holy Saturday
Prayer of Sabbatum Sanctum:
In the silence of this day my heart is stilled
The man I knew is now divine
He has left this world to be with those before
In the silence I wait .... for His return

while old friends go home with Him
In the silence, I pray that all of us
can be with Him, in paradise

April 12, Sunday
John 20:1-9 ~ To See and Believe
At some point, a Christian truly begins to believe in their heart in a living risen Jesus. It may come spiritually, by helping the poor, reading the Word, or perhaps during a Eucharistic moment. For the beloved disciple's heart to be filled, all it took was to see the burial cloths; lifting him to mystical heights. For Peter it was just a few hours later. As our heart moves towards love to see and believe in Jesus, the Spirit helps us to rise from death to self. In that moment, we know we must do and be more like Christ.

April 13, Monday
Matthew 28:8-15 ~ Great Joy!
Both Mary's example of love must have been why they were the first people contacted by our Glorified Jesus. We get a glimpse of them filled with filial fear and great joy in a spiritual embrace known as a Divine Touch that occurs even today especially in deep prayer. Can you hear the echo of them announcing the Good News of a risen Christ to the disciples? Like them, we can increasingly be a witness to Divinity's Grace transforming hearts into the color of this love.

April 14, Tuesday
John 20:11-18 ~ Our On-going Transformation
If Mary Magdalene cannot perceive that a gardener can be Jesus, how are we expected to look at anyone and see Jesus? If Mary had held onto the un-ascended resurrected Jesus, then how would we too know Christ Glorified? If we are to truly know the truth of the Word and Eucharist, we must let go of our interior desires so Jesus may ascend from within. Further still, doesn't our on-going transformation into disciples happen because of our participation with the Trinity of Father, Son, and Holy Spirit?

April 15, Wednesday
Luke 24:13-3 ~ My Heart Burns with Love
When one of my daughters was very young she made a foam Cross with the words "He is Alive" glued on. In a fatherly act, I put it above the white board

in my office. No one has ever questioned it belonging there. When I glance at that Cross, I am transformed into her innocent eyes to realize my heart burns with love for my family and Jesus. I feel blessed to be reminded at work that Jesus continues to break bread with all believers because He is Alive.

April 16, Thursday
Luke 24:35-48 ~ Touch and See
Yes Jesus, today I am going to push aside the distractions of the world to touch and see you in every person with great joy. In my prayers today I ask for Your help to: Recognize You everywhere. Help to open my mind to the peace of Your forgiveness. Let me remain immersed in the understanding of Your Word. Condition me to be a humble witness and giver of Your unconditional love. Remove all fear of the unknown. Further strengthen my faith.

April 17, Friday
John 21:1-14 ~ His Abundance
Have you ever considered returning to your old ways because Jesus's presence seemed distant? This darkness felt as spiritual abandonment affected even Peter who despite previously seeing the Glorified Jesus decided it was time to return to fishing. Yet, Peter begins to recognize forgiveness (despite his denial) filling him spiritually and precisely with numerous fish (Graces) without breaking the net. Peter's lesson includes sharing his abundance from Jesus who desires us to likewise do and be.

April 18, Saturday
Mark 16:9-15 ~ Into the World
"Go into the whole world and proclaim the Gospel to every creature." I get a tear of joy whenever I recall the memory of a moment with Christ when I agreed to try. If my heart had not been slowly softened and my belief in the risen Christ not strengthened, all traces of my humble attempts to do and be as Christ asks would not exist. Can you trace back your on-going transformation from "of the world" to "into the world?"

April 19, Sunday
John 20:19-31 ~ The Holy Spirit Transforms from Within
I had witnessed miles of metal shacks, so called homes, a harbor filled with

marginalized boat people, and deep mining cuts into the earth leaving behind wounds that would never truly heal. At an evening meal at L'arche, I saw Jesus smiling at the table. The Holy Spirit transforms from within; to change who we are, so that we can help carry peace, love, and hope, into the pain.

April 20, Monday
John 3:1-8 ~ Spirits Whispering Sounds
I am often confused like Nicodemus, but willing to listen and understand what it means to be born of water and spirit. In Baptism, we are born again to freely choose to embrace Spirits wind. Holding on can take us beyond our wild imaginations in varying intensity of coming and going. Constantly renewed, we can fail, and then rise above each time, how can we not be amazed? Knowing the Spirits whispering sounds is the Kingdom of God surfacing within.

April 21, Tuesday
John 3:7b-15 ~ Participating in Eternal Life
To believe we are born of the Spirit is to believe God as Trinity is inside. We also know that the Holy Spirit, Jesus and the Father cannot be separated. At the same time we believe that Jesus has ascended into Heaven. This wondrous and mysterious reality means if Trinity is within and Jesus is in Heaven then we are touching the entire community of divinity. This can only mean that Heaven is not some future event, but that we are already participating in eternal life.

April 22, Wednesday
John 3:16-21 ~ The Truth of God's Love
In the words of St. John of the Cross, "The Blessed Trinity inhabits the soul by divinely illumining its intellect with the wisdom of the Son, delighting its will in the Holy Spirit, and absorbing it powerfully and mightily in the unfathomed embrace of the Father's sweetness." The world needs to see us walk with wisdom, delight, and in Trinity's embrace, that St. John so eloquently speaks of, so that God's light can drive back darkness to reveal the truth of love.

April 23, Thursday
John 3:31-36 ~ Believe and Accept
The minds of every person that has ever lived, those currently living, and

whoever will ever live in the future, cannot even begin to fathom what the Father has given Jesus. My thoughts are but a drop in Jesus's unlimited ocean of thoughts. Yet, we can believe and accept the wondrous whispers from Jesus, the Holy Spirit, and the Father that guide us on our journey towards eternal life. Our gift to God in return, strengthens our resolve to receive and give even more love.

April 24, Friday
John 6:1-15 ~ Fulfilled by Jesus
The highlight of the loaves and fishes miracle for me is when the boy, influenced by the Holy Spirit, volunteers food to Andrew. I suspect the boy's faith informed him that the meager amount of food would be multiplied. His innocence, love, mercy, and compassion for his community should be our response to the needs of the physically and spiritually hungry crowd. We are to be this boy; letting our faith inform others with our joy of being fulfilled by Jesus.

April 25, Saturday
Mark 16:15-20 ~ Proclaim the Good News
I have to keep reminding myself that there is an order to what Jesus ask. Believe and be baptized then go into all the world to proclaim the Good News. In our continuing belief, if we use Jesus's name in faith and love there will be signs. However, these signs are not the goal. The world desperately needs saving and to know Jesus's embrace. Jesus will work with us as witnesses within our own journey as we become a humble drop in an ocean of hopeful drops.

April 26, Sunday
Luke 24:13-35 ~ My Heart Burns with Love
When one of my daughters was very young she made a foam Cross with the words "He is Alive" glued on. In a fatherly act, I put it above the white board in my office. No one has ever questioned it belonging there. When I glance at that Cross, I am transformed into her innocent eyes to realize my heart burns with love for my family and Jesus. I feel blessed to be reminded at work that Jesus continues to break bread with all believers because He is Alive.

April 27, Monday

John 6:22-29 ~ Works of God
Our task is to believe in what Jesus asks so that we may perform the works of God. Belief produces an upward spiral of physically doing and spiritually being for others. To support us further, Jesus supplies Himself as food for this journey. The walk towards eternal life among other things requires that we must also discern and use our individual gifts. If we humbly do so, we will see the works of God as the result of our belief.

April 28, Tuesday
John 6:30-35 ~ Bread of Life
How close we become to Jesus, ties directly to the essence of spiritual hunger and thirst. The more we live the Cross, the more we can comprehend and accept that this hunger and thirst motivates us to serve others. Jesus desires that we participate in letting other know that there is dormant love within, ready to spark into flame for each other. He is the bread of life for our society so desperately in need. We must trust that His glorious and heavenly beautification through us can transform our world.

April 29, Wednesday
John 6:35-40 ~ Believe what is Imagined
A committed Yes means we do not turn back, we allow God's will to surface and believe that what is imagined can materialize from apparent nothingness. Thirst and Hunger becomes satiated with Christ as our trusted companion. Daily trials and tribulations become minimized to become lessons in the journey. We must pray, love, forgive, and hope not just for self but others. As our courage grows, we learn to walk fearlessly towards eternity.

April 30, Thursday
John 6:44-51 ~ Life of Jesus Within
In the Catholic Mass, the Liturgy of the Eucharist begins with gratitude offered to the Father during the Eucharistic Prayer. This is followed by the Communion Rite, starting with the Our Father. When we participate in Holy Communion, we acknowledge the Father's heavenly role in the indescribable beauty of Transubstantiation. In the closing prayers, we ask for the benefits of the eternal life of Jesus within to remain active and among other things believe that He will bring us to the Father.

MAY 2020

May 1, Friday

Matthew 13:54-58 ~ Put Aside Unbelief

I can recall the feelings of a reunion of a friend where many years had passed since our last conversation. When the in between time turned to accomplishments, my memory of the person made what they became seem impossible. I should have had joy for them but instead unbelief distracted me. A significant lesson for me is that I continue to need to put aside unbelief when Jesus invites me to have faith, love, compassion and joy in ministry situations as they occur.

May 2, Saturday

John 6:60-69 ~ Holy one of God

"Many returned to their former way of life, because they could not accept what Jesus said." The reality of growing in faith requires a movement of the heart towards fully accepting Jesus. As more depth is explored, our beliefs must also increase. We cannot do it alone; it takes supernatural gifts from our Father, granting us the grace to pursue the difficult walk with Jesus. To fully understand this truth requires us to believe we are living tabernacles for the Holy one of God, Spirit and the Father.

May 3, Sunday

John 10:1-10 ~ Listen for His Voice

If you have never been around sheep you know that they bond very closely to their master. For example, when their master calls their own flock, the sheep will instantly go to the master even if his sheep are mixed in with another master's sheep. If we have truly fallen in love with Jesus then we are ready to listen for his voice, ignoring all the other distractions mixed in around us. To reflect Jesus's love to those around us is the path and gate to a life not of things or for self, but instead grace for others.

May 4, Monday

John 10:11-18 ~ Guided by the Good Shepard

A few years ago, my computer crashed due to a virus that lead to a slow and painful recovery that took more than a week. No doubt, prayer, quality time with my family, and my ability to be a sensitive business owner had been disrupted. Yet, an inner voice whispered to me, "Get up, Jerry" (Acts 11:7). Christ knows me well; evil began to lose its power and could not win when faith is integrated and guided by the Good Shepard.

May 5, Tuesday
John 10:22-30 ~ Greater than all Else
The gift of Jesus is greater than all else for us because once received, Christ cannot be snatched away. Humility is one of the clues that you are maximizing this gift. Do you avoid sitting at the head of the dinner table? When praised do you briefly smile or say thank you, then move on? Do you pray for or help others without any expectations? Do you ever make a claim about how great you are? The people in your life should know that you like Jesus do not need to.

May 6, Wednesday
John 12:44-50 ~ Glorious Fruit
Have you dared attempt to allow the Holy Spirit to work through you when you were in the world? Are you kind, just, righteousness, compassionate, loving, and consistent in prayer to help bring those of the world out of the world? This is what Jesus is asking of us. He mingled with those of the world and some came to believe. After letting ourselves mature, if we help grains (others) fall and germinate on holy ground, glorious fruit will be visible.

May 7, Thursday
John 13:16-20 ~ Receiving Trinity
Accepting the I AM of Jesus, is inclusive of receiving Trinity as The Father, Son and the Holy Spirit. Trinity inside among other benefits increases our desire to be "God like." This interior movement of our heart humbles us to bow down to freely wash other's feet and seek out opportunities to show our mercy, compassion, and love. Our virtues rise to the surface pushing aside vices that might otherwise hold us back from hearing and knowing Jesus.

May 8, Friday
John 14:1-6 ~ Christ is Where We are
Horizons are a fascinating faith concept. Depending on the environmental conditions, it can seem that as we approach a horizon, it approaches us or

sometimes a horizon moves away and we move with it. The horizon is seemingly just slightly out of our touch but obviously in our view. As a metaphor, isn't heaven there but we are not quite yet fully aware of the view of the dwelling place Christ tells us the Father has for us? Mystically, if Christ is where we are; are we not already touching heaven as we move with him?

May 9, Saturday
John 14:7-14 ~ Ask Christ for Anything
After nearly five decades of casual belief, the truth is that miles into a forest walk I challenged divinity shouting "Jesus, show yourself"! Falling to my knees, certainties deep impression gently called to do as Christ would do. Over time, divinity challenged back, confirming that to believe that works "greater than these" were possible, so that the indwelling Son can glorify the Father. When we ask Christ for anything, we become not just witnesses, but participants.

May 10, Sunday
John 14:1-12 ~ Greater Works than These
Horizons are a fascinating faith concept. As a metaphor, isn't heaven there but we are not quite yet in the dwelling place Christ tells us the Father has for us? If Christ is our way, already there; are we not almost touching all of it as we move with him? The challenge for you to consider is that if Christ is with the Father and Christ is inside, can you allow Christ to surface from Heaven within and through you do "greater works than these?"

May 11, Monday
John 14:21-26 ~ Jesus has and is being Revealed
John points us to Judas (not of Iscariot) to ask a wondrous question that is still frequently asked by each of us. Why not reveal yourself as you just did in the mystery of the meal? The answer may seem obvious to a believer but is it for everyone? You need to let God into your heart, then pass that unconditional love on to others. Otherwise, if you have love for just yourself as worldly people often do, it is impossible to realize that Jesus has and is being revealed.

May 12, Tuesday
John 14:27-31a ~ Soften Troubled Hearts

I am not a pessimist, however there is no doubt we live in an unsettled world. We are constantly being disrupted by the destructive power of the ruler of the world (Satan) with wars, genocide, and terrorism along with each of our own personal nuances. To conquer this, Jesus, the Holy Spirit and the Father as Trinity unconditionally soften troubled hearts, filling us with peace, love, healing grace, compassion, and mercy.

May 13, Wednesday
John 15:1-8 ~ He Abides in Me
When I walk through a forest in prayer, my heightened senses focus on avoiding stray branches in my path. WhenI mow my lawn, I am concentrating on looking down. I get lashed all the time by the tall side growth on the edges, as they demand to be cut back. A self-lesson has surfaced; in faith-filled situations, I am aware of Christ's presence correcting my deficiencies, but in other times, remembering He abides in me is more distant.

May 14, Thursday
John 15:9-17 ~ Share in Christ's joy
Continuously holding in our heart the mystery of Jesus as our friend, strengthens our ability to treat everyone as friends. If we are filled with Jesus's all-embracing and unconditional love, then our human weaknesses will not get in the way of letting this love flow to others. I pray that the world sees the evidence of Christians asking for and trusting the Father in Christ name. We share in Christ's joy when we naturally allow and acknowledge this grace to surface from within.

May 15, Friday
John 15:12-17 ~ In Jesus's Name
We are Jesus's friends and our friendship can mature and blossom over time. Unlike other friendships, letting His spiritual mystery grow in our hearts requires us to treat everyone as friends. Filled with selfless love (agape), our human wounds (previous emotional experiences), and weaknesses (judging, etc.) will both help us and not get in the way. A fruitful sign is that "other's" needs are satiated when we trust the Father's will or pray in Jesus's name.

May 16, Saturday
John 15:18-21 ~ Help Reveal Christ

Over the years, my straddling to be *in* the world for ministry, and *of* the world for business has changed to being *in* a majority of the time. The signs are evident such as needing to walk away from certain conversations and preferring solace in prayer. For even the strongest Christians a complete exit from *of* the world is rare. Despite the harsh reality of the necessary struggles, the Master's desire is that we remain "in" to help reveal Christ to those who yet to know Him.

May 17, Sunday
John 14:15-21 ~ Reveal Myself to You
Jesus's promise to reveal Myself to you and fill us with the Spirit of truth also reveals your ministry to transform the world. When you read the Word and consume Eucharist you believe that Jesus is no longer some external unseen thing but instead has risen from inside making you aware of Trinity's reality. Trinity's shape is like a Mobius strip: unconditional love humbly looping back through you to reflect it into your community.

May 18, Monday
John 15:26 - 16:4a ~ Moment of Surrender
As a teenager, I came close to stumbling into spiritual gluttony, nearly reducing Spirit, Christ, and Father to the point of separation, but fortunately I realized this was a disruption towards an integrated life. I now wear a Trinity Cross as a reminder that I must testify to impossibilities that only faith can explain. The side effect of witnessing is that the "other side" constantly attempts to destroy the moment of surrender and immersion into Trinity's unconditional love that we freely share.

May 19, Tuesday
John 16:5-11 ~ The Fullness of Christ
When hear the word advocate, we think of someone who supports us. The same Spirit that consoles can also expose the rawness of our participation "in the world." The unmasking of our sins can feel quite uncomfortable. However, when we allow the advocate to help us spiritually judge our self, we become "as a child" and can finally understand wrongs and are led to righteousness. This truth comes with the effect of also knowing the divine embrace of the fullness of Christ.

May 20, Wednesday

John 16:12-15 ~ Declare my Faults
My experiences have made me certain that I cannot bear the truth about myself and the world without the Spirit's help. I have accepted and dare to believe the Spirit hears my inner self speak, lets me see the truth of evil, encourages me to declare my faults, and guides me during a necessary lifelong refining process. I have noticed that when I ignore the Spirits subtle movements, there is more uncertainty and the Father's light through Jesus glorified is darkly veiled.

May 21, Thursday
John 16:16-20 ~ Rejoicing in Christ's Unconditional Love
As we more deeply to understand Jesus's rising within us, the greater we know the joy that fills us. Necessary in this cycle is an interior processing and dealing with the world's effort to defeat us. For some, the relentless hammering represents sharing a fractional portion of Jesus's journey of pain, weeping and mourning. Very few will understand how this willingness to do so, also yields a rejoicing in Christ's unconditional love.

May 22, Friday
John 16:20-23 ~ Ah Sheer Grace!
To quote St. John of the Cross, "One dark night, fired with love's urgent longings, ah, the sheer grace!" John of the Cross speaks tenderly of a second challenging spiritual night, as God seems to be missing. Yet within, hidden purifying grace transforms us with a new hunger, a taste of love's perfection, all is gained, not lost. Like a then climb towards joy with God to give it all away. Ah sheer grace!

May 23, Saturday
John 16:23b-28 ~ Reshaped into Wholeness
If we embrace an interior life there is a constant up and down cycling. One moment Jesus may seem dramatically present, then feelings of abandonment might surface. There are times when very little is understood, then a flood. There is anguish as imperfections become unmasked, then great joy and peace. There is eureka of great belief when we choose to surrender and walk with Christ. We learn to leave behind worldliness so we may be reshaped into the wholeness intended by the Father's love.

May 24, Sunday

Matthew 28:16-20 ~ Reshaped into Wholeness
If we embrace an interior life there is a constant up and down cycling. One moment Jesus may seem dramatically present, then feelings of abandonment might surface. There are times when very little is understood, then a flood. There is anguish as imperfections become unmasked, then great joy and peace. There is eureka of great belief when we choose to surrender and walk with Christ. We learn to behind worldliness so we may be reshaped into the wholeness intended by the Father's love.

May 25, Monday

John 16:29-33 ~ Peace and Courage
There is more than meets the eye when Christ speaks. Prayer such as Lectio Divina helps to unwind His living words. I perceive He speaks of evil's true intent, which is to scatter and separate us from God and each other so we cannot be loving brothers and sisters. In the subtleties of these deceits, we must remember that Christ is offering to embrace us with gifts of peace and courage to help deal with worldly struggles.

May 26, Tuesday

John 17:1-11a ~ Continue Jesus's Work
Jesus offers a prayer of gratitude to the Father for the disciples, as Jesus knows He influenced them to follow Him. Jesus, as One in the Trinity, knows that because of love, the disciples also participate with the One. If we follow Jesus, then the ripple of Jesus's prayer joins us with the original disciples to divinity and the Father's protection even as we remain in the world. To be in the presence of the Lord's Glory strengthens our own discipleship to continue Jesus's work.

May 27, Wednesday

John 17:11b-19 ~ Sanctified
When my mother was un-expectedly dying, we had a lifetime of conversations in one day. Among the many topics my heart melted when she said how grateful she was to the people in her life, how happy she was and how she looked forward to heaven. Christ protected her, filled her life with friends, love, grace and joy. Jesus's prayer to the Father was fulfilled for her. I have witnessed many others who while "in" the world lived the word. Jesus's presence obviously protected and sanctified them.

May 28, Thursday

John 17:20-26 ~ Introduced to the Father

Jesus's prayer to the Father includes us as believers in an infinite rippling effect. Spoken directly without parables, His desire is the perfection of all into an inclusive union with God. To be part of divinity is not sometime in the future but in the immediate reality of joining Jesus in the here and now. Jesus has given us what we need to do so in the form of a door opening to the spiritual sense of Glory. Our invitation is to walk through this door with Him so we may be directly introduced to the Father.

May 29, Friday

John 21:15-19 ~ Follow Me

To love as St. Peter is a challenge, especially knowing in scriptural hindsight that Peter suffers in the end. All this energy Peter put into loving God, serving others with mind, body, and soul then to suffer; how could this have been worth it? The truth of Christianity is that we are to witness Glory, to do and be like Peter and share the Cross despite the significant challenges. Accepting a sacrificial belt calls us beyond where we may go on our own if we agree to Jesus's "Follow Me"

May 30, Saturday

John 21:20-25 ~ Jesus' Volume of Books

I have made the same mistake as Peter, continually learning that uniqueness is for others to share in. The formula is simple: Jesus loves me, I can rest with him, and I need to remain with him. Do I desire what Jesus ask of anyone else or for that matter know the details of Jesus's plan? Instead, I need to recognize that we are individually filled in different ways with the same joy of Jesus's wonder. Each of us is a book in Jesus's volume of books that John speaks of.

May 31, Sunday

John 20:19-23 ~ The Holy Spirit Transforms from Within

I had witnessed miles of metal shacks, so called homes, a harbor filled with marginalized boat people, and deep mining cuts into the earth leaving behind wounds that would never truly heal. At an evening meal at L'arche, I saw Jesus smiling at the table. The Holy Spirit transforms from within; to change who we are, so that we can help carry peace, love, and hope, into the pain.

JUNE 2020

June 1, Monday

Mark 12:1-12 ~ Jesus as a Living Parable

Jesus quotes David the Palmist of God reshaping what was unworthy into a cornerstone. God knows what will become great, peace filled, or loved outside of our understanding. If we reject someone without fully understanding their purpose in life or if our judgement of a situation is clouded by unsupported supposition, we have not accepted Jesus as a living parable. Personally as I have incorrectly rejected someone, yet with forgiveness, the Lord continues to reshape me.

June 2, Tuesday

Mark 12:13-17 ~ Integrate Life and Faith

Is Jesus asking us to look at our day's wages and God as two faces in our day? One is worldly and the other is the time, talent or treasure spent with or for God. One is under obligation, the other free will. Why is there this constant tension within this struggle? Perhaps these faces of the day should not be treated as separate. While in the world, a better question is to ask ourselves is; are we ready to integrate our life and faith so that we may give God and neighbor what is God's?

June 3, Wednesday

Mark 12:18-27 ~ God is Living Here

Jesus confirms that God is with the living. St. Paul further reinforces that Trinity is inside each of us. If God is inside, how can heaven be some far away concept? How can we even imagine the fullness of Heaven in an earthly understanding since we do not know the mind of God? If God allows, we can get a glimpse within deep contemplative prayer. Any time we feel our spirit has touched divinity, should see that Heaven is not beyond reach because faith tell us that God is living here!

June 4, Thursday

Mark 12:28-34 ~ Not Far from the Kingdom of God

To love God, self and neighbor with our heart, mind and strength is well within touchable reality. I believe that our soul is hidden deep within unless we willingly participate with Trinity. The Holy Spirit breaths and animates our soul together with the entire nature of the self we know well, into union with God. This combination of our entirety and with loving neighbor places us "not far from the kingdom of God" both on earth and in Heaven here and now.

June 5, Friday
Mark 12:35-37 ~ To Learn our Own Dualities
Jesus as the Messiah places himself both as Lord to David and son of David - Son of God and son of man (Mary). As sons and daughters of God and man, He has prepared us in the delighted crowd to witness the Old Testament fulfilled and to expect that Evil will be defeated in His death and resurrection. As servants we are joyful that we have a great king not of this world. As witnesses filled with the Holy Spirit we are to learn our own dualities merged into one.

June 6, Saturday
Mark 12:38-44 ~ Filled with Gratitude
Jesus expects the scribes as teachers, lawyers and judges of the law (as he would of everyone), to give of themselves in responsible percentages for others. To humbly and selflessly give of time, talent and treasure is a sign of Christian maturity. True human wholeness like the poor widow, is to be at the service to others without the expectation of being measured or compared. I am filled with gratitude that many are turning to Jesus for guidance on distributing their abundances.

June 7, Sunday
John 3:16-18 ~ The Father's Sweetness
As I started to reflect on the Gospel reading, St. John of the Cross's thoughts on Trinity came to mind. His description of God's love trumps whatever I might have said. "The Blessed Trinity inhabits the soul by divinely illumining its intellect with the wisdom of the Son, delighting its will in the Holy Spirit, and absorbing it powerfully and mightily in the unfathomed embrace of the Father's sweetness". The world needs to see us in the truth of God's love.

June 8, Monday

Matthew 5:1-12 ~ Embrace the Beatitudes

In one sweeping poetic way Jesus teaches us how to know the Heaven that is dwelling inside and how to reach the Heaven that is not here yet. Directly said, to know and practice the Beatitudes is to be saintly. To be blessed means that self-decreases, interior spiritual hunger increases, and we rely more on God. To embrace the Beatitudes defines of the path of our journey. Are they not attributes of Christ that we must assume in order to be whole?

June 9, Tuesday

Matthew 5:13-16 ~ Christ's Light

To be humble is to be modest with our own importance, not showy, and unassuming. How is it then possible to be an unhidden light, shining bright enough for everyone to see? Ah… it is gloriously doable if the light that is showing is Christ's light not our own. Jesus teaches us that people will see this light much easier if we are not boastful or hypocritical. This light is a quiet "being and doing" for God and others without expecting anything in return.

June 10, Wednesday

Matthew 5:17-19 ~ Breathed into Scripture

The law that God has breathed into Scripture must be carefully interpreted to not include what man creates outside of the Spirits inspiration. Jesus helps us with the critical thoughts of the law throughout the Gospels, which can be summarized in just a few words; Love God and neighbor. We must first love ourselves so we can help others in their journey towards Heaven. We lead by following Christ's example of love by being humble, respectful, forgiving, having compassion, mercy, and peace.

June 11, Thursday

Matthew 5:20-26 ~ Resolve Turmoil Quickly

How people behave is often shaped by their circumstance. I try to keep this in mind as I learn to minimize my reaction to an offense. In all honesty, I still have interior frustration even if I limit my outward response. In truth, it is a righteousness test, as improving how I handle myself in these situations does not come easy. I still have to remember to quickly seek Christ's help to resolve turmoil, because I know peace comes, and then I can forgive and forget.

June 12, Friday

Matthew 5:27-32 ~ Cast Off a Vice

We have to remember that Jesus is always exploring the depth of who we are and how much further we need to go to be like God. Isn't it possible that with the subjects of increasing adultery and easy divorce, that Jesus is reaching past the surface of fidelity into everything it applies? Praising God for the beauty we see in another can instantly transform inappropriate desires. Making room for appreciating the truth of the gift of wonder and awe within that beauty can cast off a vice, effectively thwarting the other side.

June 13, Saturday

Matthew 5:33-37 ~ Disrupting Commitments

We are body, mind, spirit, and soul. Jesus wants us to firmly hold onto to this truth by keeping the elements together that make us whole. If we are not truthful, we are effectively disassociating various part of ourselves. We need to consider that our promises (oaths) always include soul, so if we shake hands, (body) only in partial agreement, (mind) without prayer beforehand, (spirit) we are disrupting commitments we make to God (via our soul).

June 14, Sunday

John 6:51-58 ~ Recognizing Sacrifice and Love

When we consume Eucharist, we are asked to believe beyond human understanding and comprehension. To just look at the Cross is not good enough, we must join the reality of Christ's mingling with our true self. Our constant invitation to become aware of Christ's on-going presence is the beginning of our being eternal. Our life lived from the Cross (with our eyes and through his eyes) means recognizing sacrifice and love rippled outward is not in vain.

June 15, Monday

Matthew 5:38-42 ~ Christ's Peace within the Cacophony

In an intense moment of pure evil, I did not react. God's responded with an instant miracle gift reversing a writing learning disability. Thomas Merton quotes: "If you write for God, you will reach many men and bring them joy. If you write for men, you may make some money and you may give someone a little joy and you may make noise in the world, for a little while." I was to anonymously witness in a noiseless joy of my ongoing conversion, reflecting on the moments of Christ's peace within the cacophony.

June 16, Tuesday

Matthew 5:43-48 ~ Love's Perfection

We are filled with love from the Word, Eucharist and witnessing God's promise to us. We cannot forget that even for those without this heightened awareness, Grace rains down equally. Willingly receiving Trinity's love begins with the responsibility of transcending negatives that come our way. Deeper still, God can break the bonds that hold us back from true wholeness. We are free to believe that Jesus inside, as love's perfection, is there for us to unconditionally give it all away to everyone we encounter.

June 17, Wednesday

Matthew 6:1-6. 16-18 ~ God is Man's Beautifier

What Jesus speaks of reminds me of a haunting verse from the song "Grace"; "Grace makes beauty out of ugly things. Among other things, private prayer and fasting exposes the interior unknowns of the ugly things of our heart and mind to consider. Our Father's response to our prayer and secret sacrifices can yield generous wisps of undeserved Grace far beyond our ability to humbly express its joy. For me, this is proof that God is man's beautifier.

June 18, Thursday

Matthew 6:7-15 ~ On Earth as it is in Heaven

Years ago, Fr. Joe enlightened me with a discussion of "on earth as it is in heaven." I suggested that there was not a hard line between heaven and earth and to my surprise he agreed. He said that the Father through Christ has made Heaven already "partially" here, but not fully revealed. For a few examples: we can perceive a taste of heaven when we sense God's presence, consume Christ in Eucharist or Word, engage the wonder of the cosmos, and hear the words I love you and then love back.

June 19, Friday

Matthew 11:25-30 ~ The Color of Love

How can I show the Father how grateful I am for Jesus in my life? Perhaps if I could fall down in delight, awe and praise more often, learn to listen for the Lord even in the worldly cacophony, forgive where forgiveness seems unworthy of the moment, embrace when it feels like the last thing I would ever do and, let Jesus take me to a pain free place, then maybe, just maybe I could fully encounter the heart of Christ; a heart the color of love.

June 20, Saturday

Luke 2:41-51 ~ Looking for Jesus

If our Christian bearings point us towards the Father's house how can we ever be lost? When I was a teenage boy, I got lost running though forest trails in a long-distance running practice. My parents started looking for me because I was four hours late. However, I knew what to do, I went to the tallest hill, climbed a tree to get my bearings and walked straight to where they were. It seems the answer to prevent being spiritually lost, is to always be looking for Jesus.

June 21, Sunday

Matthew 10:26-33 ~ To all You Encounter

In the contemplative tradition the word dark has a different meaning. Dark means an undeniable faith hidden away from all else where only God's love is present. Within the dark, the Spirit speaks in ways that only you can understand, invisible to the prying eyes of the other side. What becomes infused within then belongs to all you encounter. As long as you allow the virtue of prudence to also rise to the surface you can share what has been given without any fear.

June 22, Monday

Matthew 7:1-5 ~ Judgmental and Hypocritical

Lord, praise you for letting me see the truth of how easy it is for me to be judgmental and hypocritical of other's faults. Through these you have made it possible for me to one by one become aware of my own faults that need interior reflection and correction. While quite painful, I pray and desire that you continue to let me uncover and change my hidden natures. I know the list remains very long, but I trust you will help me pick them off one by one, no matter how small.

June 23, Tuesday

Matthew 7:6, 12-14 ~ The Narrow Gate

Since youth, whenever disturbances come at me from all sides, I seek the quiet of the woods. God's grandeur surrounds me, rocks and roots are invited to uncross in my path, and turmoil dissipates. When I leave a worn forest trail to pray deeper, Christ blazes a new way, traceless, and beyond my control. Firmly on holy ground, the narrow gate opens to views such as dew on spider's webs behaving like strings of pearls. Another battle won, Trinity fills me with peace, love and joy for others.

June 24, Wednesday
Luke 1:57-66, 80 ~ Hands and Feet of Jesus
If you are a parent, I am sure you know the blessings of a child. Circumstance played a part in naming of one of my children. As each child was born I felt truly blessed, reminded again by people at my children's Baptism and now as I observe each child throughout their lives. I am sure like me you are constantly amazed how they are the hands and feet of Jesus, spreading their strong wings to bring beauty into the world.

June 25, Thursday
Matthew 7:21-29 ~ Give our Received Grace Away
To be a Christian means active participation of what others might call coincidences, but we know them as the whispers of the Father's will for us. These moments create an unshakable foundation of faith superseding our human nature. Despite life's buffeting, the grace of faith lifts us up, yielding praise and gratefulness for God. Grace builds upon grace, and we have no choice but to make sure we give our received grace away.

June 26, Friday
Matthew 8:1-4 ~ Knowing Leprosies
There are many times in my life that I feel "clean" such as after a good confession, a sincere prayer, a silent walk into nature, during Mass, helping others, and a focused conversation with my wife. With all the effort I put in, it would seem remaining clean would be easy. Yet, my life with Jesus is like a roller coaster, as I constantly rise then fall into knowing leprosies so my experiences can teach me how to humbly offer an outstretched hand to the crowd.

June 27, Saturday
Matthew 8:5-17 ~ Less Than a Breath Away
If you are a Roman Catholic in the U.S. you are familiar with the short prayer said just before communion: Lord, I am not worthy that you should enter under my roof, but only say the word and my soul shall be healed. We believe the Lord does say the word, if we become the Centurion then our souls have eternal life. The Lord, from this distance of less than a breath away, with all the request of the cosmos to consider, is going to respond to

our request.

June 28, Sunday

Matthew 10:37-42 ~ Jesus Mingling Within

Have you ever thought about the different kinds of love you might have? Is your love of your spouse, parent, child, friends and your hobbies the same? Have you ever thought about their order? Where is God in your hierarchy of love? Jesus challenges us to have God above all which is easy to do if you consider Jesus is actually inside. By filtering out the reality of Jesus mingling within of His presence, power and sacrifice we deny our reward.

June 29, Monday

Matthew 16:13-19 ~ Thank you Jesus!

Like he did for Peter, Jesus Christ my savior has held out His hand to save me from not fitting into a world filled with temptations, drowning in my sorrow, selfishness, anger, pride, greed, and even denying God's existence, yet, here I am; deeply in love. This would not have been possible without the rock of my Church community. When I walk through those metaphorical doors, I feel humanity mingle with divinity to lead or follow in order to serve others. Thank you Jesus!

June 30, Tuesday

Matthew 8:23-27 ~ To Know Christ Better

I have personally felt the closeness of physical death numerous times in my life. I know grace and prayer saved me each time. At 50, I mysteriously looked directly into the reflection of my worldliness to experience a different kind of death; a death to self. More than a decade has passed since that moment. Christ inside has continued to calm wave after wave of intense personal storms. My response is to trust and know Christ better, so through me, He may touch the lives of others.

JULY 2020

July 1, Wednesday
Matthew 8:28-34 ~ Selfless Choice
The story of Jesus driving out the swine is increasingly appropriate for the deeper worldliness we have progressed into within the last decade. The fact that the whole town wanted him to leave because of what he had done is a striking metaphor. Yet, I have personally witnessed instances of evil being perished because the lens of selfless choice was used. With the gift of fearlessness, we can accept Jesus's embrace and learn to walk away from those who outright reject true love.

July 2, Thursday
Matthew 9:1-8 ~ With Jesus's Authority
Christian journeys often include an "ah ha" moment when Christ inside is truly recognized and the desire to become like Jesus willingly begins. You can recognize it when you cooperate with Jesus's authority, easily forgive others and apologize for transgressions. It also becomes obvious that previous issues must be resolved to be whole. While sometimes painful, we deeply explore and accept our human faults letting Jesus turn these negatives into healing joy.

July 3, Friday
John 20:24-29 ~ Doubting Thomas
Years ago, I wrote a poem titled "Doubting Thomas". Despite the weakness of my faith at the time, I knew God had a path for me. It leads off with the first stanza "Small Wire" a poem by Anne Sexton.

"My faith
is a great weight
hung on a small wire,
as doth the spider
hang her baby on a thin web"

Then transitions to my own stanza of "Doubting Thomas"

My light faith as the spider strand metaphor,
sways in the breeze, barely holding onto me
So thin, even a breath can push it far away
I wonder if I can be like her greater weight

July 4, Saturday

Matthew 9:14-17 ~ Unexplored Territory

Attempting to live the Christian life is filled with inconsistencies. Sometimes we must embrace what we already know and behave within whatever constraints, customs and traditions that may exist. Other times we are in unexplored territory where everything is new and we must be prepared for anything. In this case, our challenge is not to fit the square block into the round hole but to discern the required shape, then with Jesus's help allow our transformed self to enter.

July 5, Sunday

Matthew 11:25-30 ~ The Color of Love

How can I show the Father how grateful I am for Jesus in my life? Perhaps if I could fall down in delight, awe and praise more often, learn to listen for the Lord even in the worldly cacophony, forgive where forgiveness seems unworthy of the moment, embrace when it feels like the last thing I would ever do and, let Jesus take me to a pain free place, then maybe, just maybe I could fully encounter the heart of Christ; a heart the color of love.

July 6, Monday

Matthew 9:18-26 ~ Jesus Can Work Through Us

Sandwiched within the story of Jesus raising the official's daughter from death, is the woman in the crowd who in faith touched Jesus's cloak and was healed. As a Christian we know that as we make our way towards something, we are often presented with an opportunity of an unexpected encounter. These can be looked at not as interruptions but proof points that Grace has and will be there. In these moments we are called to be present so that Jesus can work through us.

July 7, Tuesday

Matthew 9:32-38 ~ To be a Laborer

In my attempt to live an integrated faith, I cannot help but notice that in every facet of life there are many who seem spiritually lost. I am moved to do something about it. I have struggles to deal with like everyone else, but I know Jesus has my back. One of the ways to be a laborer, is to act and believe in the truth that God as Father, Son, and Holy Spirit desires our help to ease physical and spiritual hunger and suffering with compassion, mercy, peace, and love.

July 8, Wednesday
Matthew 10:1-7 ~ Contemporary Apostle
Starting with twelve disciples who each focused within their own community, Jesus created a lasting ripple. If we advance forward in time and place to each of us as apostles full of Grace, we are challenged to continue the ripple outward to strengthen those who already believe, find the lost, and spread the Good News. Helping Jesus reveal the Kingdom that is already here but not fully unveiled is our mission as contemporary apostles.

July 9, Thursday
Matthew 10:7-15 ~ Our Own Ripples
There is no doubt that St. Francis of Assisi followed Jesus's words to perfection. Filled with Grace, love, and peace, Jesus became present wherever St. Francis traveled. I personally know humble people in my community who proclaim the Good News, pray and do good deeds, all the while remaining silent, needing nothing in return. Like them, we are all uniquely invited to awaken to Heaven's reality so that like St. Francis we may leave behind our own ripples of Jesus's love as we journey with the Lord.

July 10, Friday
Matthew 10:16-23 ~ Let Trinity Speak
Faith requires a lot from us especially if God is asking us to be present for others even in the worst of times. In these situations, it is hard push back our own opinions and let Trinity speak through us. My own tendency is to want to soften the blow of what should be said. Unfortunately, what we have heard God speak in our hearts, unconsciously becomes charged with our own feelings. Noticing these influences is the first step towards resisting our own thoughts and trusting the Lord.

July 11, Saturday
Matthew 10:24-33 ~ To all You Encounter

In the contemplative tradition the word dark has a different meaning. Dark means an undeniable faith hidden away from all else where only God's love is present. Within the dark, the Spirit speaks in ways that only you can understand, invisible to the prying eyes of the other side. What becomes infused within then belongs to all you encounter. As long as you allow the virtue of prudence to also rise to the surface you can share what has been given without any fear.

July 12, Sunday
Matthew 13:1-23 ~ Sowing in Good Soil
As someone who wears hearing aids, Jesus's explanation of the sower parable takes on special meaning. It would seem not hearing very well would reduce distractions so I can listen for Jesus speaking to me. However, when you have a deficit in one sense you often get an increase in others. I can smell odor a great distance away and clothing can be irritating. Yet, God is mercifully helping me learn how to push through "noises" so I may assist in sowing in good soil.

July 13, Monday
Matthew 10:34 – 11:1 ~ Jesus's Sword
When I was a child, I understood evil as large in scope, such as the threat of an atomic bomb. Now, I know evil is sneakier, hiding not only in my own thoughts, but also in those of family members, friends, and strangers. Jesus's sword can help us cut away the part of us (or them) that we discern is evil without hurting what we love, strengthening, and growing our connection to divinity. To do so we must also encounter the Cross as a follower of Jesus.

July 14, Tuesday
Matthew 11:20-24 ~ Awakened to Unconditional Love
I am an example of Christian choice. As a child, God had invited me to not only repent but to be inwardly prayerful and do outward for others. At the time I did not understand the call. For decades I remained what I would call an adequate Christian. Then, during prayer immediately after 9/11, in an unexpected moment with Christ, the desire for internal transformation overpowered my entire being. I was awakened to unconditional love from deep within, and the yearning to let it flow outward.

July 15, Wednesday

Matthew 11:25-27 ~ Inspired to Love Unconditionally
To know the Father is to also know Jesus and the Holy Spirit. How well do you know each? What has been revealed to you beyond the Word you hear proclaimed, the receiving of Eucharist, your praise in prayers, your ability to understand but still accept? If you are inspired to love unconditionally as a child might, you believe and trust in God, and you are grateful, then you are already "knowing" Trinity. This sense of being orientated correctly is just one example of grace from the Father.

July 16, Thursday

Matthew 11:28-30 ~ Make Our Burdens Light
It would not be appropriate to ask Jesus to carry the weight of all our problems. For instance, we cannot expect difficulties at our jobs to be miraculously resolved, as clearly, most belong to us. Instead, I believe Jesus speaks of the many flavors of evil that surround, tempt, distract, and push us down spiritually. We must strive to completely trust that Jesus's embrace will hold these at bay so we can rest in his love and peace to make our burdens light.

July 17, Friday

Matthew 12:1-8 ~ Rest on Sabbath
I have yet to figure out how to completely rest on Sabbath. After Mass, I might work in the church garden or spend some time with family. Sometimes unfinished Saturday chores such as mowing the lawn creep into Sunday afternoon and our chickens need daily care. I hold onto the fact that it is a day of thanksgiving. I try to pray throughout the day and just be as much as possible. Sabbath has always taught me that I need to reflect on the mercy of the Lord.

July 18, Saturday

Matthew 12:14-21 ~ We are all Beloved
For decades, I wondered what it would feel like to be fulfilled all the time instead of in just brief burst. I had not yet connected the dots that true fulfillment comes from desiring Christ's embrace. I now realize fulfillment is especially victorious when it includes "the other." Truly accepting Christ's within has filled me with hope and cured me of that feeling of un-fulfillment. I am certain God is delighted with my progress and we are all beloved even with our failures and weaknesses.

July 19, Sunday

Matthew 13:24-43 ~ Jesus is Tending You.

If you believe that the Holy Spirit and Jesus is inside you, then since God is Trinity, the Father must also be inside. If Trinity is in Heaven then the Kingdom of Heaven must at least partially be inside. Allow yourself to explore this thought; God gave us Jesus, isn't Jesus God, isn't God everything? To help you grow Jesus is tending you, and embracing you with joy and unlimited love. You are the wheat in the field, you are the mustard plant and, you are in the Kingdom of Heaven!

July 20, Monday

Matthew 12:38-42 ~ Something Greater Ahead

This Scripture passage reminds of a U2 song titled "Wave of Sorrow." Its haunting lyrics reference the Bible passages of the Queen of Sheba visiting Solomon for his wisdom along with an interpretation of the Beatitudes. The song is a reflection of Bono and his wife Ali being present to the suffering during the Ethiopian famine. The song awakens a sense of mercy, hope and the future of something greater ahead. These feelings remind me that Jesus within is our inspiring sign.

July 21, Tuesday

Matthew 12:46-50 ~ The Will of our Father

My family is my community, my rock, and the place I can go for many of my needs. I have a close spiritual family, stretching out to church, and to those who believe as I do. My spiritual community of brothers and sisters continues outward to those who have left their earthly bodies behind. I know they pray that Grace may allow me to further open my heart to the will of our Father further expanding my family horizons to total strangers I have met and yet to meet. I desire to comprehend this expanse.

July 22, Wednesday

John 20:1-2. 11-18 ~ I have seen the Lord

I am sure like me that if you have lost a loved one, you occasionally experience brief moments of that person's spiritual existence throughout your life. You might perceive a gentle touch, vivid thoughts, or memories that reassure you that person is with God in Heaven. If we allow it, these moments of not holding on to the physical past can strengthen our beliefs in Divinity. Like Mary we can understand enough to say, "I have seen the

Lord."

July 23, Thursday
Matthew 13:10-17 ~ Comprehend Jesus's Parables
Our human minds must first surrender so that our hearts may heal and comprehend Jesus's parables. If we do so, God attempts to reveal the mysteries of the Kingdom of Heaven to everyone who will listen. With it comes the responsibility to act and "be" according to what has been given. The more we understand, the more we learn to allow God's Grace to flow through us to those who need it. The true measure of this acceptance to perceive, listen, be and do what we receive is growth in humility.

July 24, Friday
Matthew 13:18-23 ~ Jesus Working Through Us
It seems fashionable to think at the moment of death one will enter Heaven because of God's mercy. However, if Divinity is inside, doesn't that mean Heaven is already present in the here and now? Why miss out on this peace, joy and love within? We need to persevere through the daily challenges and distractions that come between us and living in Jesus's presence. The fruit of our relationship becomes visible when we witness Jesus working through us in the doing and being present for others.

July 25, Saturday
Matthew 20:20-28 ~ Reshaped as Chalice
"My chalice you will indeed drink." This chalice, while overflowing with love, does come at a cost. Paraphrasing St. Paul, Jesus is in our body, manifested in our mortal flesh. No doubt we are God's containers. Our hearts are able to fill abundantly with the Father's grace in mercy and compassion. As we become reshaped as chalice we must also join with Christ and others to suffer and serve as ransom. Difficult as it seems, to serve as vessels means participating in the mystery of the Cross, while Grace within ripples outward.

July 26, Sunday
Matthew 13:44-52 ~ We are the Pearl
We are precious to God, he has found us and surrounds us with love, peace and joy. To immerse ourselves with Jesus, what we know partially continues towards the full reality of the Kingdom of Heaven. To Jesus, we are the pearl of great value as treasure hidden in a field. With our "Yes", we are being

renewed as God separates us from evil. Imagine for a moment that God "sold" Jesus his only son, to be on the Cross for our salvation.

July 27, Monday
Matthew 13:31-35 ~ Mystery of the Kingdom
One could argue that if Jesus was here now physically in our world using modern day parables there would not be the need for explanation. However, with a knowledge of farming and making bread, it still took me years to understand and begin to accept all that goes with the reality of being the yeast with Jesus inside. How much of your old self has decreased to allow Christ to multiple the size of the dough so that the mystery of the Kingdom of Heaven becomes present for others?

July 28, Tuesday
Matthew 13:36-43 ~ Fields of Weeds
As a business owner, I know of unrighteous fields of weeds and various flavors of evil. The feeling is unsettling, as along with dealing with my own sins I must battle external ones. Work environments easily create situations where if I am not careful I can be drawn into assisting evil by wounding others. I am learning that my daily prayers need to include asking for Christ's light to settle my own nature and create compassionate corporate souls.

July 29, Wednesday
John 11:19-27 ~ If I Had Been There
If I had been there! There have been many times in my life that I have I felt that if I was not somewhere else I could have prevented something from happening. I no longer think that way. I now know it is a selfish thought primarily because I am not God. What I offer now to the "could have been situation" is my love, mercy, compassion and a prayer asking Jesus for a good spiritual resolution as I know it will be given.

July 30, Thursday
Matthew 13:47-53 ~ Transform from Old to New
We can only go so far with our own skill set to transform our old self to new. The hard stuff requires special handling by God and through Graced helpers. As willing Christians, we can be reshaped like the potter to the clay or like a seamstress recasting the mother of a bride's wedding dress for her precious daughter, the new bride. Like the bride surrendering to the expert, the balance

of reforming our old self prepares us for the Heaven we do not yet know.

July 31, Friday
Matthew 13:54-58 ~ Put Aside Unbelief
I can recall the feelings of a reunion of a friend where many years had passed since our last conversation. When the in between time turned to accomplishments, my memory of the person made what they became seem impossible. I should have had joy for them but instead unbelief distracted me. A significant lesson for me is that I continue to need to put aside unbelief when Jesus invites me to have faith, love, compassion and joy in ministry situations as they occur.

AUGUST 2020

August 1, Saturday

Matthew 14:1-12 ~ Seduction by the Dance

We are witnesses to the seduction and appeal of the "dance" across the globe in the form of wealth, drugs, and bodily perfection. However it is our free will to instead practice the dance of true love when Trinity is the center of our being. To surrender to love can counter all earthly desires, heighten righteousness, increase humility, allow spiritual freedom, and willingly accept persecution. Filled with Trinity's love we carry St. John's thought of making way for the Lord into the world.

August 2, Sunday

Matthew 14:13-21 ~ Reflect Jesus's Love

When I wrote this reflection, I was comfortably settled under a canopy of pines overlooking a pond at a large conservation property with a small cabin. This "deserted place" has turned into a once a year retreat. It was my 40th wedding anniversary and I was transfixed by the gift of my wife. In the prayerful experience, I noticed continued self-transformation, as despite my own needs I prayed deeply for her. I still need to consistently reflect both mine and Jesus's love back to her.

August 3, Monday

Matthew 14:22-36 ~ It is Time to Accept

We often ignore, abandon, or have doubt about gifts from God that do not seem to fit who we think we are. Ah… but Scripture tells us that Jesus gives Peter multiple opportunities to "walk on the water" (the gift of faith). Even after denying him, Jesus asks, "Do you love me" and with his "Yes" Peter becomes the Rock of many miracles. In the back of your mind, I am sure like me you have denied multiple offers from Jesus to get out of the boat. Perhaps it is time to accept.

August 4, Tuesday

Matthew 15:1-2, 10-14 ~ Gladly Explain Parables

If you ask anyone to explain any one of Jesus's parables you will likely get something different than your own explanation. As a person who lives less than a mile away from a cow farm I know exactly what the expression "the barn door is opened" means along with many other suburb expressions. I gladly explain them to my friends who live closer to the city. Shouldn't we gladly explain parables and also listen intently for explanations of Jesus's parables to potentially hear something we did not know as there may be something for us in it.

August 5, Wednesday
Matthew 15:21-28 ~ Give a Needed Crumb
Have you been interrupted by someone that needs help especially when you were tired? Maybe you were also hungry and thirsty. Deep inside you knew you must raise them up because they need a morsel of healing with spiritual food, perhaps just a portion of what you have. Like Jesus, when you give a needed crumb, grace embraces the "other." Yet, unlike Jesus, we must be careful to rest in-between, so that grace can fill us and remove our visible weariness.

August 6, Thursday
Matthew 17:1-9 ~ You are God's Beloved
The transfiguration is one of those scenes that that we all seem to have a similar visualization. Was this mystical experience a one-time event, arranged just for Peter, James and John? When you place yourself with them, doesn't the Word come alive; don't you see Jesus in the dazzling light and, hear the Father speaking? Do not be afraid of your own experience of consolation, you are God's beloved son or daughter, with whom He is well pleased.

August 7, Friday
Matthew 16:24-28 ~ Life in Christ
Jesus is not just talking about our personal sufferings, there are also the crosses of not fitting into a world filled with temptations, belonging to a small percentage who prays often or being a Christian guided by Trinity within. The list goes on but our "yes" means we must never give up and often go against the tide. Our whole self must embrace God's will, using Jesus's example to lead or follow as necessary, and serving others, if we are to find life in Christ.

August 8, Saturday

Matthew 17:14-20 ~ We are the First Mountain

Three decades ago for a short time with my job, I flew first class, purchased whatever I wanted and believed I could do anything I desired. I had not realized that I was lost. The faith to move my mountain started with love by those close to me. With their prayers, Jesus rebuked the wrong inside me. The impossible through Christ is very real to me because my own faith in Him has moved mountains. Being far from perfect, we are the first mountain that needs moving.

August 9, Sunday

Matthew 14:22-33 ~ Accept in Faith

We often have doubt about the reality of gifts from God that seem unusual for us. Sometimes we ignore or do a trial run, then abandon them because they may require effort. Ah… but Scripture tells us Jesus gives Peter an opportunity at the extraordinary by walking on the water. After several attempts with his lessor faith, eventually Peter does permanently accept Jesus's offer. Perhaps like Peter your doubts should dissipate and accept in faith.

August 10, Monday

John 12:24-26 ~ Glorious Fruit

Have you dared attempt to allow the Holy Spirit to work through you when you were in the world? Are you kind, just, righteous, compassionate, loving, and consistent in prayer to help bring those of the world, out of the world? This is what Jesus is asking of us. He mingled with those of the world and some came to believe. After letting ourselves mature, if we also help grains (others) fall and germinate on holy ground, glorious fruit will be visible.

August 11, Tuesday

Matthew 18:1-5, 10, 12-14 ~ Allow Jesus to Find You

The world entices us with convenience, pleasures of all types, the desire to possess, and a different definition of love than we knew when we were innocent. To me the parable of the lost sheep is reversed in today's world, as the ninety-nine seem lost, not the one. It is virtually impossible to not want what the ninety-nine have, unless like a child we are willing turn to Jesus to speak in our human voice "here I am Lord." Allow Jesus to find you.

August 12, Wednesday

Matthew 18:15-20 ~ Desire for Restoration

A broken relationship that needs healing first begins with our unconditional open heart in honest gentile conversation. Our desire for restoration must include hope for wholeness and mending the harm, otherwise the wound remains both in them and us. Jesus and the community of saints want to help so bring Divinity in with your prayer beforehand. We should only give up conversion when it becomes impossible but prayer for the relationship should never cease.

August 13, Thursday

Matthew 18:21 – 19:1 ~ The Lord's Mercy

Lord, soften me with grace so I may be at peace, let me taste moments of deep forgiveness. Let my heart be the color of love so others know a mark of Your touch. I am ready for a final confrontation of several more painful past hurts so that I may be cured forever. I must fall to my knees more often, forgive where forgiveness seems unworthy, embrace when it feels like the last thing I would ever do, then maybe, just maybe I will understand the Lord's mercy.

August 14, Friday

Matthew 19:3-12 ~ A Voice from the Desert

Have you ever heard the cry of a voice from the desert? It can be startling and beautiful at the same time. To respond as if it the only thing we have left to do is not easy because the depth of obligations that goes with it slowly gets revealed. As we learn to accept what is asked of us, God will make our path straight. Then at the right time we will be prepared for the metaphor of the winnowing fork throwing the wheat into the air to separate out the grain from the chaff.

August 15, Saturday

Luke 1:39-56 ~ To Magnify the Lord

My heart has leap for joy at the expectation of childbirth, receiving Eucharist and in the encounter of a faith filled Christian. The Holy Spirit's prompting creates an invitation to talk, become brother or sister, pray together, help recognize Christ in each other, and to magnify the Lord. This offer of Mary and Elizabeth to each other, to be blessed and to bless God, is the fruit possible from our unique spiritual wombs.

August 16, Sunday

Matthew 15:21-28~ Give a Needed Crumb

Have you been interrupted by someone that needs help especially when you were tired? Maybe you were also hungry and thirsty. Deep inside you knew you must raise them up because they need a morsel of healing with spiritual food, perhaps just a portion of what you have. Like Jesus, when you give a needed crumb, grace embraces the "other." Yet, unlike Jesus, we must be careful to rest in-between, so that grace can fill us and remove our visible weariness.

August 17, Monday

Matthew 19:16-22~ Giving up Much

I will never forget a Mass when without any disruption, an intellectually disabled young man walked the length of the aisle so he could touch a newly baptized baby. It was electrifying when the baby's parents gracefully reached out to him. I wanted to do the same. I continue to thank God for those involved in giving up much of themselves so this wonderful young man could unconditionally love us. We were all born again in that moment.

August 18, Tuesday

Matthew 19:23-30 ~ At Peace and Hopeful.

To deny desires beyond what is adequate creates space that God values and fills with Jesus's love. It is a circuitous process as when we reach negatively across the line our internal agape weakens and our human wants rise to the surface. There have previously been numerous times in my life that my connection to Divinity had been weakened. In retrospect although I felt on top of the world, love had slipped away. I trust God now, I am more at peace, hopeful, and know this foretaste of heaven.

August 19, Wednesday

Matthew 20:1-16 ~ Watching Many be First

It took me decades to understand that instead of being envious I needed to be joyful whenever I encountered God's grace at work in others. So too was the moment in my late 40's, when I accepted Jesus's equal and unconditional love halfway through my "day." I will be thrilled to be at the end of the line watching many be first because everyone deserves to be fed even if it only comes at the end of their day (life).

August 20, Thursday

Matthew 22:1-14 ~ Wearing the Garment of Christ

God widely broadcast the invitation to heaven here and now. With so many other choices the invitation is lost to many. Curious, others come seeing just its surface then leave as it does not appear sufficiently desirable to pursue. Some begin to dance, abandoning the invitation because unmasking our personal layers of vices is painful and challenging. To stay long enough to enjoy the feast requires preparation, endurance, letting go, gratefulness, and wearing the garment of Christ.

August 21, Friday

Matthew 22:34-40 ~ Revealed Mysteries

Christ affirms the truth of the prophets: to love God and neighbor. Scripture as the inspired word of God further reveals this truth in written form. What remains for us is to be enlightened by this truth. Do not be surprised when your interior life, actions, the Word, Eucharist and prayer further reveals and multiplies the desire to love God and neighbor. In St. John of the Cross's words: "Even in our time God... grants manifestations or declaration of already revealed mysteries."

August 22, Saturday

Matthew 23:1-12 ~ Cast Christ's Love Outward

I wear hearing aids to help with a humbling hearing loss. The replacement (un)gift is sensitive skin that is always conscious. But, ah... the hidden Rosary around my neck has to only slightly move to remind me that Christ is present wherever I may be. We each live with our own burdens, but unseen grace lifts us up. Isn't it appropriate that we should not seek false love, but quietly cast Christ's love outward from within?

August 23, Sunday

Matthew 16:13-20 ~ Thank you Peter!

Jesus Christ my savior, has held out his hand to save me from drowning in sorrow, selfishness, anger, pride, greed and even denying God's existence, yet, here I am; deeply in love. This would not have been possible without the rock of my Church community. When I walk through those metaphorical doors, God is silently waiting to embrace me, rescue me from my sins, nourish me, and to confirm my humanity mingles with divinity. Thank you Peter!

August 24, Monday

John 1:45-51 ~ Become Still

Am I following God in the way that is expected? My mind is crammed full of ideas, full of things I must do and I have so little time. Yet, in this split second within a breath, I recognize a flaw - I am being duplicitous, I often make my own path without first "sitting under the fig tree." Instead, I must constantly glance at the radiance of Christ and heaven that is touchable only by believing. A Monk repeating Jesus's words once said to me that to see greater things I must become still.

August 25, Tuesday

Matthew 23:23-26 ~ Conflicts Inside of my Cup

Our world disturbs and alarms me, yet, how am I to be judged if I am not part of its transformation? I have to constantly ask myself if have "neglected the weightier things of the law: judgment, mercy, and fidelity." St. Augustine states: "Our hearts are restless until they rest in Thee, O Lord." I must first be caught up in a whirlpool cleansing conflicts inside of my cup so I may rest, otherwise how can I be and do outside of it.

August 26, Wednesday

Matthew 23:27-32 ~ Emphasizing Humility

Ah... Jesus is again emphasizing humility. What good am I if I wear my faith as if it is a uniform filled with awards and badges? I cannot have pride in anything especially in my call to ministry as I am only unique as everyone else, not special. If I appear as a know-it-all then I am no different than those who put Christ on the Cross. Instead I must strive for a simpler life, as one in which others visibly see in me Christian love.

August 27, Thursday

Matthew 24:42-51 ~ Even Before Death

As one grows in the spiritual life, the forces of universe that are not God attempt to tamp down our beliefs and the deepening moments of faith that surface from within. Jesus directly speaks to the ability to awaken your heart to Him, not sometime in the future, but right now. He is inviting you to join in with the living reality of the communion of saints. By participating in Heaven that we can grasp in the present time, prepares us for its infinite breadth and depth even before death.

August 28, Friday

Matthew 25:1-13 ~ Fully Realizing Heaven

Christ's kingdom of heaven is not a distant future event but current reality inside and unique to each of us, beginning at his incarnation. His metaphors point to the invitation to be people of God, a life filled with oil of the Holy Spirit and graces that we use wisely. We pursue the clues of the Father's will that manifest in various times and places. Becoming more aware of Christ, Spirit and Father mingling with our self, we begin to sense a slow unveiling of heaven.

August 29, Saturday

Mark 6:17-29 ~ Satan Get Behind Us

Like the generations of Biblical "Herod's", evil continues to influence the need for some to have total domination, creating situations in which innocents fear for their life. It is complex moral issue because the answer is not always fighting fire with fire. We are not without hope as our Christian obligation is to cry out for God's mercy. As a crowd of two or more, in memory of John the Baptist and others, in Jesus's name we pray; "Satan get behind us".

August 30, Sunday

Matthew 16:21-27 ~ Set Your Mind on Divine Things

Peter needed help to see that self and evil had penetrated in his journey with Jesus. We suffer from the same problem as Peter with our crosses of not fitting into a world filled with temptations, belonging to a small percentage who prays often or being a Christian guided by Trinity within. To set your mind on Divine things means our whole self must embrace God's will with Jesus's help and example, leading or following as necessary, and serving others, as we have found Christ.

August 31, Monday

Luke 4:16-30 ~ The Spirit of the Lord is Upon Me

In Jesus's time, the Sabbath day brought everyone to pray at the Synagogue where any adult could read from the Torah and provide a sermon. Jesus stood in front of town's population of an historical estimate of 400 people to read from Isaiah pronouncing the short sermon of "Today this scripture has been fulfilled in your hearing." We have to ask ourselves the simple question of shouldn't we be able to proclaim, "The Spirit of the Lord is Upon Me?"

SEPTEMBER 2020

September 1, Tuesday
Luke 4:31-37 ~ Ask to be Cleansed
Almost three decades ago, I had not realized how far I had drifted away from the center of being a good Christian. Full of pride I walked down a dock crowded with boat people living in extreme poverty, the instant shame within was as if a fire. Turning to Jesus, I asked to be cleansed but unlike the man in this story, removal is still happening in increments. Jesus's plan lets me see and experience my own demons, which like chameleons change color and shape in order to hide until routed out.

September 2, Wednesday
Luke 4:38-44 ~ Trinity and Heaven are Weaved Within
Jesus, Paul, and generations of others before us, as we should also, proclaim the good news that the Kingdom of God has and continues to arrive with Christ at the center. The Holy Spirit fills us with courage and faith to believe Jesus's mission goes beyond restoration to include His introduction to the Father so we may witness (in actions, words and prayer) Trinity to others. Reaching inward, we know that Trinity and Heaven are weaved within the fabric of our lives.

September 3, Thursday
Luke 5:1-11 ~ Amazed at the Catch
Jesus's fishermen casting nets for people has yielded over 2 billion Christians. There have been historical periods where we have been amazed at the catch. I am personally seeing faith that is deeper, more voluntary, and informed. This renewed welcoming is born from the early Church, understands that the Word is alive, embraces the Holy Spirit, accepts Christ within and is filled with Grace, forgiveness, mercy, compassion, joy and love.

September 4, Friday
Luke 5:33-39 ~ Allow Yourself to be Filled
Fifty years ago, I used a metal canteen that kept getting dented to quench my

thirst when I went on forest hikes. Now, I use a nearly indestructible plastic bottle. They are a metaphor as both were necessary in my journey, as I need Grace that that brings me to my knees and Grace that fills me with joy. We are God's receptive containers; allow yourself to be filled and transformed with the appropriate Grace pouring out for others within the moments we are in.

September 5, Saturday
Luke 6:1-5 ~ The Lord's Grace
I have a weekday routine that includes prayer before going to work. Sabbath is more intense, as my obligation is to prepare myself to respond to spiritual hunger. This is the day people seem more receptive to the Lord's Grace. Being filled with Jesus, God intentionally creates encounters for you with "the other" who may need a smile, compassion, encouragement, reassurance of their value and appreciation of the wonder of loving God and neighbor.

September 6, Sunday
Matthew 18:15-20 ~ Desire for Restoration
A broken relationship that needs healing first begins with our unconditional open heart in honest gentile conversation. Our desire for restoration must include hope for wholeness and mending the harm, otherwise the wound remains both in them and us. Jesus and the community of saints want to help so bring Divinity in with your prayer beforehand. We should only give up conversion when it becomes impossible but prayer for the relationship should never cease.

September 7, Monday
Luke 6:6-11 ~ Bring Joy to the Other
My wife and I do whatever we can to reserve Sunday afternoons for ourselves. It's our way of extending the morning past Mass being with and loving the Lord. Conversations afterwards but before leaving the church building, then walking into the world filled with this love is our way of loving neighbor. We intentionally seek the many choices of quieter places so we may be restored and where our authentic, sincere asking of neighbor; "How are you doing?" can bring joy to the "other."

September 8, Tuesday
Matthew 1:1-16, 18-23 ~ A Special Kind of Love

To be a father of a yet to be born child, who you know is not yours, takes a special kind of love. Men, think about this for a moment, would you do it? Could you be Joseph? Would you have to be filled with righteousness and the grace and love of the Lord to do so? These glorious "Yes(s)" occur every day and everywhere around the world. Would it fill you with joy to hear the media announcing these "Good News" interventions? God bless these men.

September 9, Wednesday
Luke 6:20-26 ~ Rippling Love
From my backyard I can watch the rising sun cast a subtle beam of light over golden tassels of corn. My senses consume with great joy the beginnings of the new day. This is the same taste that I hunger for throughout the day, but it is elusive. Within an hour or so, I will exit this wonder to enter a world filled with poverty, sadness, anger, intolerance, and selfishness. Lord, let your glory bless and overwhelm me, rippling love through me to those in need.

September 10, Thursday
Luke 6:27-38 ~ Gift of Love
Genuine love is metered out equally without prejudice. Although an impossibility in physics, the echo of the love returned is greater than it began. Our love must reach into places it has never been if we expect to make changes in our world. Our personal gift of love may not be able to end a war, but perhaps it may settle an argument, change a sinner's heart, or heal an inner wound. Our reward will be more love than we could ever imagine, echoing it outward by sharing its gift with others.

September 11, Friday
Luke 6:39-42 ~ Serve in Worthiness
Today, I am going to work hard to resist a quest for power, to compare myself to others or desire anything. Instead, I will strive to listen, to see joy where there seems to be none, to look interiorly and move to be last in line. Perhaps in this on-going surrender, I will see the unrecognized flaws in myself. As I become weaker, I know Christ will mend what is flawed, fill me with kindness, peace, love, and understanding so in Him I may serve in worthiness.

September 12, Saturday

Luke 6:43-49 ~ Treasure in our Hearts
Consuming Jesus in Eucharist and Word builds up the treasure in our hearts, we become "activated" and Jesus patiently waits for our "Yes" to surface. As a personal metaphor, to have a notion of Christ presence, try to discipline your breathing for a few seconds. We don't realize it but inhaling and exhaling is not a conscious act. Eventually, like breathing, the desire to be and do His will becomes automatic. Your faith creates an impenetrable wall to evil, permeable to all else.

September 13, Sunday
Matthew 18:21-35 ~ Softened by Grace
Not so long ago, I knew I had to fall down to my knees more often, forgive where forgiveness seemed unworthy, and embrace when the battle inside said not to. As I began to do so in faith, I have encountered the heart of Jesus, a heart the color of love. In these brief moments, I have been softened by grace to receive the kind of love, peace, and joy that last for eternity. To know true forgiveness, I must allow the confrontations of my own will to be superseded by eternity's light in the darkness.

September 14, Monday
John 3:13-17 ~ Merciful Eyes of Jesus
Despite the violence that surround us we believe that Jesus has saved the world. We have to remember Moses's Seraph in the desert - one had to look at it after being bitten (sins) to be saved from death. Although by God's Grace over time, our sins may have grown smaller, we continue to be bitten, this is why salvation is more than one time saying, "Jesus is my Savior." As believers, like Nicodemus, we have to constantly remember to look directly at the merciful eyes of Jesus to ask for forgiveness.

September 15, Tuesday
John 19:25-27 ~ An Encounter of Love
No doubt Jesus must have developed a deep friendship with the disciple he loved for many reasons. The most humanly tender reason for me is that He knew Mary would need someone she trusted to continue to love and care for her as He did. The gift to the disciple He loved was an encounter with the mother of God that no other human would ever experience. Do you treat your mother, your significant other's mother, or friend's mothers as a new loving experience?

September 16, Wednesday

Luke 7:31-35 ~ Without Judgment

My parish has a variety of ministry groups that provide prayer, love, food and basic necessities to others expecting nothing in return. To take part in any of these groups is a decisive action, bringing joy when it is time for happiness and weeping in times of sadness. As children of the Father, brothers and sisters of Jesus Christ, and receivers of the gift of wisdom by the Holy Spirit these ministries humbly know to do so without judgment.

September 17, Thursday

Luke 7:36-50 ~ Demonstrate your Love

Have you ever gone to a function where you know there are others who have an opposite viewpoint? Did you avoid them? Jesus did not; he entered the home of a Pharisee who obviously did not have Jesus's best interest in mind. So did the sinful woman with her precious oil, publicly humiliating herself with her loose hair, tears, washing and kissing Jesus's feet. How far would you go to demonstrate your love of God and others?

September 18, Friday

Luke 8:1-3 ~ Offer a Grateful Prayer

It is natural to believe the resources of the women followers of Jesus was money, however given the historical timeframe, I am sure it included planning, other human essentials and prayer, as Jesus and his twelve disciples traveled villages proclaiming the Good News. If you have someone providing for you, especially if it is with their thoughts and prayers, take a moment and offer a grateful prayer to them and to Jesus for their grace.

September 19, Saturday

Luke 8:4-15 ~ Personal Parables

I woke before dawn, instantly being aware that after reading scripture and prayer I was supposed to hike a very particular narrow trail, despite heavy fog. Everything seemed to slow me down, roots came out of nowhere, the trail was nearly invisible, it wound in on itself, and branches slapped me in the face. Exiting the forest onto prepared ground added to my list of personal parables. If I persevered and endured difficult challenges, faith would yield even more. What of your own journey?

September 20, Sunday

Matthew 20:1-16a ~ Watching Many be First
It took me decades to understand that instead of being envious, I needed to be joyful whenever I encountered God's grace at work in others. So too was the moment in my late 40's, when I accepted Jesus's equal and unconditional love halfway through my "day" (life). I will be thrilled to be at the end of the line watching many be first, because everyone deserves to be fed, even if it only comes at the end of their day.

September 21, Monday
Matthew 9:9-13 ~ Empathize with the Heart
When I look around, I see myself as one in a crowd of many who are in need of a spiritual physician. To let Jesus the "physician" help make us right, requires us to step back from our worldliness. His gift leads us on a path towards purification so that mercy and compassion can rise up and out naturally. Our own healing helps us to understand how to empathize with the heart and mind of those in need because of what we have received.

September 22, Tuesday
Luke 8:19-21 ~ Just Be or Act on the Word
We hear the expression brothers (and/or sisters) when someone starts a talk in a fraternal organization, at Church and in St. Paul's letters. Jesus as Paul does is speaking to the spiritual membership of us as brothers or sisters in our own community and the body of the communion of saints. This love filled membership here on earth and the entire cosmos of God is inclusive to all who hear, then "just be" or act with the Word for anyone in need.

September 23, Wednesday
Luke 9:1-6 ~ Share Jesus with Others
Coming up on two decades ago I slipped from I will do a little, to a firm Yes with the Lord. The worldly circumstances of my life have radically changed, mostly outside of my control. I can't remember the last time I really wanted something personal. Barriers have been broken so that within encounters, my humble Christianity opens an opportunity for spiritual healing. I have no doubt that I am at ease with experiencing the invitation to share Jesus with others.

September 24, Thursday
Luke 9:7-9 ~ To See Jesus

Aren't there are times in our lives varying from when we are troubled to when we are joy filled, that we keep trying to "see" Jesus because we believe? Knowing Jesus's touch reminds us and assures us with even a little prompting that we are to share in the glorious feeling. Light reflecting outward from within ourselves helps those who want to see Jesus, combine with their own spark. It can even attract those like Herod who fear believing.

September 25, Friday
Luke 9:18-22 ~ Say Christ is Lord
Some bibles use rebuke instead of sternly ordered. Rebuke as in the other places in the Gospels, means sharp criticism. Peter's answer to the question of "who am I," perhaps needs to be reflected on, so that we come to Jesus the Messiah of God not for miracles but for the mystery of love. True love for the other is not without suffering. In your suffering, do you silently share it on the Cross and discern the moments that someone needs to hear you say Christ is Lord?

September 26, Saturday
Luke 9:43b-45 ~ Seeing Through Jesus's Eyes
Fr. Henri Nouwen passionately proclaims that we "are beloved children of God." We are also children of human parents making us human with divinity within. Our human side converts betrayal into deep emotions. We shutter when we begin to understand why God's love allowed our brother Jesus to be on the Cross. God allows us to be there also, as without seeing through Jesus's eyes, the meaning of love could not manifest to others.

September 27, Sunday
Matthew 21:28-32 ~ Faith Calls Us Forward
I know that I have frequently not done what the Lord expected from me. However, each time God's unconditional love allowed me to return to the routine of working in the vineyard. I am not alone in worldly challenges as everyone is given the chance to change their mind and come back to the Father. We just have to keep remembering that sin attracts us away from righteousness, but faith calls us forward towards belief and forgiveness.

September 28, Monday
Luke 9:46-50 ~ Jesus's Loving Response
I know people who are masters at changing the conversation if it is already

familiar to them. My inclination is to pursue the conversations depth until I understand. I suspect John knew he was supposed to divert the conversation about who was the greatest so the other disciples could let what Jesus said change their hearts. Maybe John fed Jesus this softball query so they would more easily comprehend Jesus's loving response to those using his name.

September 29, Tuesday
John 1:47-51 ~ Jesus and Heavens Presence
It has taken many years for me to realize that Jesus sees me walking towards him. Most of journey felt like I was on a roller coaster, sometimes I was easy to be seen at the top and other times difficult down at the bottom. It is in those upward movements that we realize Jesus is acknowledging us. Our roller coaster needs to change to an endless up as we climb the mountain of faith. Metaphors like climbing help us to grasp belief in Jesus and heavens presence.

September 30, Wednesday
Luke 9:57-62 ~ Comfort of Home
At a young age my wife and I purchased land for a house. We cut down trees, and after the foundation and outside of the house was up we built the rest of our home with our own hands. At the time, I did not understand my commitment to Christ could put into question the luxury and priority of this resting place. Jesus's warning to the would-be follower is personal for me as I am ready but, my "Yes Lord" as of yet does not seem to mean I have to give up the comfort of home to serve God.

OCTOBER 2020

October 1, Thursday

Luke 10:1-12 ~ Eucharist Resonates from Within

While very few of us can move from town to town proclaiming the Kingdom of God is at hand, our Yes means we are asked do so within our own community. Within mine, it is easy to notice a warm genuine thank you is more than enough payment for something some might say or do for "the other." For me personally, consuming Christ in The Word or as Eucharist resonates from within to fill me for spiritual ministries, especially when my role is to take a lead, guide conversation, or prayer.

October 2, Friday

Matthew 18:1-5, 10 ~ Re-balance selfishness and Greed

From a great distance, I have witnessed various holy people's humility. In Jesus's name, they have all spoken to today's reading, telling us there is far more that can be done to raise the lowest up. Some take these thoughts to mean capitalism and free markets are evil. Rather they, as I do, believe a radical correction is required to re-balance selfishness and greed so that loving God and neighbor comes first. If that is corrected then the lowest will be naturally raised.

October 3, Saturday

Luke 10:17-24 ~ Thank You Father

There are occasionally times when it feels like nothing can harm me because I am a worthy disciple. Yet, for the most part, I am a fragile human affected by even subtle disturbances. In these times, my habit of wrapping my fingers around the cross on my chest is the security blanket that brings peace. I hear myself spiritually saying thank you Father for this gift of a childlike touch point to remind me that Christ is with me, and just as important, in everyone I meet.

October 4, Sunday

Matthew 21:33-43 ~ To Do and Be Present

As active Christians we need to occasionally confirm that we see the signs of fruits of the Holy Spirit in our lives. Love, joy, peace, patience and many other stabilizing or growth virtues should be readily apparent. Our faith and beliefs reflecting outward helps to produce additional fruit for the Kingdom as we attract others to be Christ like. Firmly established with the cornerstone, we are meant to "do and be present" for others.

October 5, Monday
Luke 10:25-37 ~ Let your Soul be Present
For years, I thought loving the Lord and neighbor with all my being meant my physical existence. More recently, I have come to realize the deeper meaning of "with all your soul" is far more complex. For instance, prayer is one way our soul participates with divinity. We may also recognize our soul in instances of intuition. Further still is a willingness to let your soul be present and united to God so that love, mercy, and compassion can rise from within.

October 6, Tuesday
Luke 10:38-42 ~ Our Life Aligns with Jesus
As someone who has deeply mourned, it was easy to notice those who had comforted me and thank them. At the same time, there were others, who behind the scenes, had done things that were not as visible. This does not mean I did not appreciate them. Later, when I felt better, I also acknowledged my gratitude to them. In the same way, while we may not notice Jesus, if we pay attention, peace becomes present, and our life aligns with Jesus.

October 7, Wednesday
Luke 11:1-4 ~ Strength to Endure
I find it curious that Luke tells us that one of the disciples ask Jesus how to pray as John taught not as Jesus had just done. Jesus's response is a prayer that John as a Jewish man would be mostly comfortable with. For Jesus the Father is not a metaphor, but a reality. When was the last time you truly acknowledged that the Father is holy, invited the Kingdom to be present, and asked for bread that satisfies both hungers, participated in two-way forgiveness, and requested strength to endure?

October 8, Thursday
Luke 11:5-13 ~ Mutual Persistence
I was extremely grateful and fortunate to have had a spiritual director (a

priest) for well over a decade. Without even knowing such a person existed, the Holy Spirit searched my heart, finding and placing him into my life. I distinctly remember when a single word from him triggered a waterfall but our mutual persistence helped control the flow. Over the years, our relationship has changed to now being good friends who with a knock will be there for each other.

October 9, Friday

Luke 11:15-26 ~ Armor Against Evil

In my restlessness, in my desire to change the world, what do I "hear," distractions to do this or that, or rather grace in the form of pure peace, love and charity of God? These gifts are armor against evil, shaped as a compassionate smile or in words, cast towards someone in need, ablaze in my eyes. I must let Christ's love ripple in my actions today as both defense and offense in the constant second subtle and sometimes-stronger wave.

October 10, Saturday

Luke 11:27-28 ~ Illuminate His Word

Imagine if you can, re-entering your mother's womb knowing her warm embrace. Here, the troubles of the world dissipate, your senses are limited, colors are pale, sounds are muted, and you cannot speak. Stay there in prayer for a moment, sense the touch of Christ's loving light, and open your ears to illuminate His Word, remain silent to let the moment of rest bring you peace.... let that peace remain as you exit to enter the world again.

October 11, Sunday

Matthew 22:1-14 ~ Wearing the Garment of Christ

God continuously broadcast the invitation to the heaven of here and now. With so many other choices the invitation is lost to many. Curious, others come seeing just its surface, then leave as it does not appear sufficiently desirable to pursue. Some begin to dance, then abandon the invitation because the required process of unmasking personal layers of vices is challenging. To stay long enough to enjoy the feast requires preparation, endurance, letting go, gratefulness, and wearing Chris's garment.

October 12, Monday

Luke 11:29-32 ~ Listen to Wisdom

You may have asked for a small sign from God. If God was generous, you may have received a feeling that all will be well, peace, warmth from within, or perhaps a sense of increasing faith. Classically, one of the lasting effects of these acknowledgments is the desire to identify and judge interior wrongs. These accumulating moments can result in ongoing multiple conversions. If you listen to wisdom, you can grow in certainty that Christ must be present now, in the past, and into the future.

October 13, Tuesday
Luke 11:37-41 ~ Things That are Within
The truth of Christian faith is very simple; we must unconditionally love God and neighbor. There are no shades of gray to what this means. On one hand, we cannot live in luxury as the Pharisee did then once a week go to church assuming that my obligation to God and neighbor is fulfilled. The alms Christ speaks also include prayer, praise, service, love and faith, and allowing those things that are within to be cleaned by grace. Grace also shields us against distractions and goals of grandeur.

October 14, Wednesday
Luke 11:42-46 ~ Examining my own Faults
It is tough to put myself into Jesus's conversation as if I was one of these rigid Pharisee, but I believe that is what I am supposed to do. Why else would Luke specifically say teacher? Being far from perfect I can see myself in these and other imagined woes that Christ might say about me. I have started to learn that I should not find fault in others until I have finished examining my own faults, which I cannot possibly complete before my death.

October 15, Thursday
Luke 11:47-54 ~ Reject Hate
To emphasize and pass on truths, while eliminating the negatives that are false from our ancestors is a great responsibility. Deep in our heart we have the knowledge that Christ comes first in everything. I, like you know that it is hard to reject hate when our every emotion feels it. However, in God's wisdom we can pray to can change hostility into peace. If we can each teach the next generation how to break the cycle of vices just a little, goodness will prevail.

October 16, Friday
Luke 12:1-7 ~ Love's Value Comes First

For a couple decades it used to be that I did not even recognize some of what I did were sins. Christ had other plans for me as wrongs began to result in silently saying sorry. The hardest part of my staged journey came next with a deep sense of remorse and guilt, forcing me to wonder what God thought. The next stage was the beginning of a strong desire to go to Confession. Now, filial fear and humility make me not want to offend, believing God knows my secrets and love's value comes first.

October 17, Saturday
Luke 12:8-12 ~ Spirit's Love and Peace
When you must put yourself in front of others for God, know that you are embraced and loved by the Trinity of Father, Son and Holy Spirit. Believe in what Julian of Norwich says "all will be well." It is normal if prior to the experience you require silence, conversation, prayer, interior purgation and possibly restitution (to feel whole). For some it is best to always be ready. Do not fear because the Holy Spirit's love and peace will fill you with courage.

October 18, Sunday
Matthew 22:15-21 ~ Giving to God is Joyful
When you think about giving to God the things that are God, what are your immediate thoughts? Perhaps because of your wonderful relationship with Him, it is prayer, praise or gratitude. Perhaps it is what your do, or be for the other of spouse, family, friends or even strangers. What of the taxes? If you are like me, it is done only because it is the law, but you do not agree with where the money goes to and how it is used. Giving to God is joyful, giving taxes is with resistance.

October 19, Monday
Luke 12:13-21 ~ Collecting Spiritual Treasures
Jesus's desire for us is that we seek holy and spiritual possessions. Despite unrelenting worldly influence, we can be close to divinity by beginning now to collect spiritual treasures. This goal is not easy, as we must also allow purgation to begin long before our physical death by dying to "self" in the process. Our personal evidence is knowing that others come first in our thoughts, prayer, compassion, mercy, encouragement, generosity, joy and love.

October 20, Tuesday

Luke 12:35-38 ~ Until the Master Knocks
Years ago, I frequently traveled for business across the maximum time zones one can, typically away from home for two to three weeks. My wife prepared spiritually and emotionally for my return to give me the time and space I needed to recover. I was not as grateful as I should have been during that period of my life. The interior life revealed how devoted she was and is. Now is it my turn to serve her the best I am able, until the master knocks.

October 21, Wednesday

Luke 12:39-48 ~ Disciples of Increasing Gifts
"From the one to whom much has been entrusted, even more will be demanded." If we acknowledge Jesus's arrival in our life then allow Him to transform us, we become disciples of increasing gifts. As a disciple, we are expected to walk the walk and talk the talk of unconditional love. As we move towards fully accepting Jesus's embrace, the responsibility intensifies because we come to know the master and want to be and do anything He ask of us.

October 22, Thursday

Luke 12:49-53 ~ Anguish Yields to Love
Christ's fire within instills a unique reality that others may not understand or appreciate. Depending on how we act and verbalize our relationship with Jesus, can mean even those close to us can disagree, resent, or even be divided against us. We also know that we are meant to reflect Christ's anguish yielding to love, kindness, and peace for others (including those who are on the other side of the divide), wrapping them in mercy and compassion.

October 23, Friday

Luke 12:54-59 ~ Willingly be in Purgation
It is easy to slip into thinking that Jesus is only focusing on the human condition of settling something before it gets out of hand. The rawness of the metaphor strikes deeply at our "trespasses" of each other. Jesus is also likely speaking about our primary relationship with God. Are we are counting on settling our debts with God, only after death in purgatory? What about God's presence now, shouldn't we already willingly be in purgation?

October 24, Saturday

Luke 13:1-9 ~ Enriched Christian

God has given me numerous chances to allow grace to transform who I am so that there may be fruit from His will. In hindsight, I can see that the numerous missed opportunities to do so still outnumber the successes. However, I have come to understand that a constant attempt at forward movement is what really matters. This knowledge carries the responsibility to be present any second for others. The mark and sign of knowing we are an enriched Christian is like the fig trees fruit.

October 25, Sunday

Matthew 22:34-40 ~ Revealed Mysteries

Christ affirms the truth of the prophets: to love God and neighbor. Scripture as the inspired word of God further reveals this truth in written form. What remains for us is to be enlightened by this truth. Do not be surprised when your interior life, actions, the Word, Eucharist and prayer further reveals and multiplies the desire to discover how to better love God and neighbor. In St. John of the Cross's words: "Even in our time God… grants manifestations or declaration of already revealed mysteries."

October 26, Monday

Luke 13:10-17 ~ Healing our Self and Others

To rest on the Sabbath means allowing ourselves to be embraced in the arms of the Lord at any time, absorbing grace filled love so we may give it away. Being "busy" makes this is difficult to do. Jesus's divine view is that being distracted (by the other side) causes us to lose our focus and desire for God's love. Therefore, our well does not become filled. We need Jesus's love so that we can become unbound and healed, reflecting love others as Jesus has done for us.

October 27, Tuesday

Luke 13:18-21 ~ Transformed From Within

Heaven already partially here and Heaven yet to come can be thought of as a continuum. Jesus's death and resurrection began a process whereby with faith each of us can become part of the Kingdom already here. While we wait for God to become fully visible to the world, we can be transformed from within. As a planted mustard seed or the mixed yeast and dough, we joyfully grow in community towards what is yet to come.

October 28, Wednesday

Luke 6:12-16 ~ A Place to Pray
If I am in a situation that I must make a big decision, I try to arrange a time when I can create silence such as a long walk into the forest to have a place pray without interruption. I do so because of Jesus's example of thinking and praying about the twelve who would be spiritual leaders out of the multitude of disciples to choose from. Our prayer life is a critical element for choices in our lives. At minimum, time with divinity can bring peace for decisions.

October 29, Thursday
Luke 13:31-35 ~ Gathered into the Waiting Arms of Jesus
Christians, Christians, wouldn't it be wonderful to be gathered into the waiting arms of Jesus. Further still, believers in God could unite to reveal the sly fox's disruptions throughout the world. It is time to willing love unconditionally, be merciful, and compassionate so that we might receive and reflect the glorious healing light that the Lord desires for us. How else will those who newly enter the sphere God creates for us recognize Christ?

October 30, Friday
Luke 14:1-6 ~ Considering Others on Sabbath
Jesus no doubt emphasized Sabbath's day of rest to include the being and doing of helping others in need, celebrating being together at the table, and the company of friends and family This challenge of reaching out to strangers especially on the Lord's Day even today goes beyond what we think Sabbath is for. Yet, given that ultimately we know God is love, it makes sense. Jesus's example calls on us to consider "the other" in prayer, sacrifice and mercy.

October 31, Saturday
Luke 14:1, 7-11 ~ Faith Filled Conversation
Years ago in numerous business situations I was one of the guests of honor and unfortunately I acted that way, going straight to the host expecting I was to sit near him. In my lengthy conversion process I now prefer the posture of being very approachable, always presuming God is placing me where I am supposed to be. I have been amazed more often than not, when grace, like water taking the shape of the container, produces a faith-filled conversation.

NOVEMBER 2020

November 1, Sunday

Matthew 5:1-12a ~ The Beatitudes are Our Journey

In one sweeping poetic way, Jesus teaches us how to know the Heaven that is dwelling inside and how to enter the remainder of Heaven that is not here yet. To know and practice the Beatitudes is to be saintly. To be blessed means that our own desires decrease, interior spiritual hunger increases, and we become more dependent on God through faith and virtues. The balance of the Beatitudes are our journey; to become Christ like in order to become whole.

November 2, Monday

John 6:37-40 ~ The Fathers Will

If you believe in the living water of Christ, it becomes easier to accept the fullness of what it means to do the Father's will, especially when you eliminate the fear of the unknown. As you actively participate, what may first start as thoughts, materializes into actions and being present for others. Moving beyond the walls of what we think we know allows us to be exposed to the same thirst, hunger and love as Jesus, walking hand in hand towards eternity.

November 3, Tuesday

Luke 14:15-24 ~ Wanting the Taste of More

It seems to me that the truth is we become so busy with our own desires that we fail to understand the reality of Christ's invitation. Perhaps you have been awakened to dine with Christ's by an extreme, such as suffering, a singular life-changing event, or more subtlety recognized divinity in the beauty of a sunrise. The sign that we have accepted God's embrace, is that we will be instilled with a desire of forever wanting the taste of more.

November 4, Wednesday

Luke 14:25-33 ~ The Gift of Peace

In the years our children were going up, society opened up Sunday mornings to play community sports. My wife and I felt that Mass at Church took precedence. Likewise, I have projects I would like start, but I would have to eliminate Morning Prayer. Our Crosses would seem to disappear if we went backwards with less prayer and reduced social justice activities. It would not be worth it because the gift of peace was fleeting before my original Yes.

November 5, Thursday
Luke 15:1-10 ~ Lost and Weak
I have visited economically poor villages in multiple locations outside of the US. A couple of the noticeable observations from these encounters include that regardless of their situation people's faith was remarkably visible and their care and righteousness for each other was pure. My reaction each time was an awareness that compared to them I was lost and weak. It did not take long to realize Jesus was willing to put me on his shoulders for the journey towards what they had.

November 6, Friday
Luke 16:1-8 ~ Take Corrective Action
Although I have made great strides I am still a sinner. As God's steward, I put myself on the line such as with these with meditations that have permanence on the Web. How is it possible that my sinning and stewardship can coexist? God already knows my weaknesses and is ready to forgive if I confess, have regret, and take corrective action. I believe God thinks no less of anyone, which compels us to express gratitude and continue to try not to sin.

November 7, Saturday
Luke 16:9-15 ~ Love Requires an Open Heart
Jesus speaks to the poor and the poor of spirit as well as the rich and those rich in spirit. These are not necessarily synonymous. If you are poor or rich but generous with God's gift to you of time, talent or treasures you will be rich in spirit. To be rich in spirit comes with serving the Lord as master. I have learned that to think rich people are not generous (or willing to be) creates a wall. I know firsthand that to love requires an open heart.

November 8, Sunday
Matthew 25:1-13 ~ Fully Realizing Heaven
Christ's kingdom of heaven is not a distant future event but current reality inside and unique to each of us, beginning at his incarnation. His metaphors point to the invitation to be people of God, a life filled with oil of the Holy

Spirit and graces that we use wisely. We pursue the clues of the Father's will that manifest in various times and places. Becoming more aware of Christ, Spirit and Father mingling with our self, we begin to sense a slow unveiling of heaven.

November 9, Monday

John 2:13-22 ~ Jesus's Personal Temples

Today's Gospel reading reminds me that we are Jesus's personal temples; His tabernacle. We must do our part to keep it vice free and not allow disruptions. The holiness of our temples is not built overnight but takes a lifetime to become constructed. Our journey to recognize Christ has been and is now actually present is not always easy to recognize. The signs of this "knowing" include observing that we do not come first in thoughts or prayers and do God's will without hesitation.

November 10, Tuesday

Luke 17:7-10 ~ Mercy Within Unconditional Love

Have you begun to feel compelled to give without any expectation? If so you are in dawn of accepting God's love emerging from within, to do and be this love. Perhaps you are putting many other human desires aside to please God, knowing you have a very long way to go. To continue to grow in the accepting the reality of pleasing Trinity within attracts us toward those that have yet to know mercy's unconditional love.

November 11, Wednesday

Luke 17:11-19 ~ Prostrating for Others

Being grateful to God cannot be understated. For example, I live near a city that is #2 in the US for the worst car accidents per capita. I have long suspected this is because of selfishness. I have been on the receiving end of accidents over a dozen times and was never apologized to. Recently, I was rear-ended at high speed and the insurance company considered my car a total loss. As a Christian, I prayed for those that caused these accidents because we are expected to be one of the ten prostrating for "others" to be healed.

November 12, Thursday

Luke 17:20-25 ~ Glimpse of Heaven

If you ask your friends to describe Heaven it will likely be some future existence that has a distinct entry point. However, Jesus has already entered our space bringing Heaven within our reach. We do not need to run anywhere because when we consume Eucharist, immerse ourselves in the Word, feel deep peace, and love unconditionally we should at minimum get a lighting flash glimpse of Heaven. For now, we know Heaven through a glass, darkly.

November 13, Friday
Luke 17:26-37 ~ Cooperating with Divinity
When you look around what do you see? Are your friends and family full of love, do they care for each other and their neighbors? Do you feel satisfied with your nominal needs? Are you opening your heart to reveal Jesus? Do you allow yourself to be embraced by Trinity's radiance? If so, you are ready for whatever comes. During the waiting period, we comply with the obligation to our duty in this life, fearlessly cooperating with divinity as we traverse our eternal faith journey.

November 14, Saturday
Luke 18:1-8 ~ The Luster of Our Soul
It is likely that you have had periods within your life when your faith became weaker. Forgetting to pray is often part of either leading up to or during these times. My own experience is that this is when evil can subtly slip between the cracks to open up selfishness, pride, independence and other vices. Doubt then rises to the surface. You need to pray, even though you do not feel like it because restores and maintains the luster of our soul so Jesus can become visible.

November 15, Sunday
Matthew 25:14-30 ~ Generous use of Gifts
While we recognize, cherish, and let God's unique gifts fill our hearts with love, ultimately these gifts are meant for growing the kingdom of God. If they are not intentionally and prayerfully used, they will wither away. You may have noticed either in yourself or others that the joyful, humble, and generous use of gifts seems to result in increasing gifts as if an ever-expanding outward spiral. This is Jesus's way of saying thank you for using what has been given.

November 16, Monday
Luke 18:35-43 ~ Miraculous Gift of Faith

To allow ourselves the freedom to shout out to Jesus, "have mercy on me," is a sign we are accepting the miraculous gift of faith. With this gift, we can be witnesses to miracles that are not easily explained. The exchange often creates a desire to glorify God. I personally have a significant learning disability that retreats to the background for long moments. I can directly attribute this minor miracle to Jesus, so I express signs of gratitude, such as being a Lector or writing a daily blog post.

November 17, Tuesday
Luke 19:1-10 ~ Our own Zacchaeus Story
Like Zacchaeus, we can become aware that we may be lost in worldliness. How we respond to this realization is the key to our salvation. Salvation requires prayer, regret, restitution, seeking forgiveness, entering an examination of self, loving God and neighbor and a purgation process. Perhaps the greatest gratitude we can give is to humbly proclaim in deeds and actions our own Zacchaeus story to the benefits of others.

November 18, Wednesday
Matthew 14:22-33 ~ Accept in Faith
We often have doubt about the reality of gifts from God that seem unusual for us. Sometimes we ignore or do a trial run, then abandon them because they may require effort. Ah... but Scripture tells us Jesus gives Peter an opportunity at the extraordinary by walking on the water. After several attempts with his lessor faith, eventually Peter does permanently accept Jesus's offer. Perhaps like Peter your doubts should dissipate and accept in faith.

November 19, Thursday
Luke 19:41-44 ~ Know the Grace of Peace
Have you been visited by Jesus? Does peace wash over you with the desire to be and do beyond? Jesus's "I Thirst" is a cry out for each of us to also thirst for a community filled with love and peace. Unfortunately, this visit also yields the knowledge that the moment we step into the world we will be disrupted by forces that do not want peace. We must be strong, while also weeping at missed opportunities for others to know the grace of peace.

November 20, Friday
Luke 19:45-48 ~ Bold Like Jesus

In the business world, I can confirm I have been in a den of thieves where greed surfaces. What about dens of people who gossip? Taken in this light we can imagine other types of dens. We have to remember that we are always on sacred ground. Our responsibility is to steer towards the positive, which sometimes occurs by simply being present. Occasionally we must be bold like Jesus, but be prepared (by praying) for "death stares" or people walking away upset.

November 21, Saturday
Luke 20:27-40 ~ Children of God
The poem High Flight by John Magee begins with: "Oh, I have slipped the surly bonds of Earth...." Then ends with: "and touched the face of God." Filled with awe within the silence and sanctity of his flight he understood that while alive on earth we are spiritually children of God. Like him we can rise in our own unique way. Perhaps you can take a few minutes of silence to contemplate and be with our living God then truly believe in humility that others can witness the face of God in you.

November 22, Sunday
Matthew 25:31-46 ~ Righteousness
Not all virtues are as clear as righteousness; either you are right or you are wrong. Either you believe Jesus Christ means we must treat others as we treat ourselves or be selfish. Either we are all one in mind, body and soul or we are not. If we are never hungry, can drink fresh water anytime, have shelter, are clothed and have access to medicine; then we must attempt to bring equality with either our time, talent or treasures to others or we cannot believe we are righteous.

November 23, Monday
Luke 21:1-4 ~ Reaching out to the Spiritually Poor
Jesus seems to be speaking of the human realities of pretentiousness and wealth but there is greater depth if our integrated divinity is considered. The poor widow is also a symbol to sacrifice our whole self. What percentage of yourself are you putting into the spiritual treasury of Heaven that is now? Consider this partial list of gifts: Gratitude to God, prayer for others or gently reaching out to those that are spiritually poor including the wealthy.

November 24, Tuesday

Luke 21:5-11 ~ A Sign from Heaven
Despite the daily signs of our world seemingly falling down physically and morally, as Christians we need not be afraid. We are graced to experience the beauty and touch of Jesus's peace. When we embrace and are embraced by the Word and Jesus's light, are hearts overflow with hope and love that attracts others. We grow to understand there is only one Triune God with a desire is for us to be a sign from Heaven for our community.

November 25, Wednesday
Luke 21:12-19 ~ God's Love Conquers All
As a Christians you constantly have your faith challenged in a number of ways. It could be as simple as being influenced that reading scripture is not current, going to Church is not necessary or more complex such as spiritual angst, or even persecution. These marks of attempting to live a saintly life can be visible to you. To silently bear witness to this suffering is the best offense. We must hold strong to prayer never forgetting that God's Love conquers all.

November 26, Thursday
Luke 17:11-19 ~ Prostrating before God for Others
Being grateful to God cannot be understated. For example, I live near a city that is #2 in the US for the worst car accidents per capita. I have long suspected this is because of selfishness. I have been hit over a dozen times and was never apologized to. Recently, I was rear-ended at high speed and the insurance company considered my car a total loss. As a Christian, I prayed for those that caused these accidents because we are expected to be one of the ten prostrating before God for "others" to be healed.

November 27, Friday
Luke 21:29-33 ~ Trinity's Precious Sunlight
Perhaps from a distance you have seen the buds on the tree, or you may have even close up witnessed them burst into leaves. No matter where you are in Jesus's metaphor of your journey, God is near you. It is your free choice to consume the Word of Christ and begin to bloom. From there you can absorb Trinity's precious sunlight to refresh the entire tree, growing in love and joy in the never ending fruiting of your Heavenly relationship.

November 28, Saturday

Luke 21:34-36 ~ Gift of Strength
Contradictions are part of the interior life of a Christian. To name but a few there is emotional anxiety, all types of suffering, and forgetting divinity is within. Then there are moments of pure peace, being pleased we are on the cross, and the deep desire to get even closer to God. It requires great strength to withstand the tribulations that go with purgation when on earth. St. John of the Cross left behind a legacy of writings on the gift of strength as we stand before the Ascended Christ.

November 29, Sunday
Mark 13:33-37 ~ Keeping Awake
Is keeping awake because we do not know when our life will end, or is it really about when our life in Christ begins. I personally lean towards being ready for Jesus to suddenly have something for us to do or be for someone. Jesus doesn't normally enter our path in extraordinary ways but rather in our tender sensing of a need, most often not even our own. He places us in a situation and our job is to recognize the master wants our help.

November 30, Monday
Matthew 4:18-22 ~ Jesus Thirst for your Love
Jesus continues to walk along calling out to each of us. I am sure you know someone whose life was radically changed because they heard and followed. For them, is it often difficult to put into words what they feel. It can be so strong they must give up a portion of their current life (or for some all of their life) to serve God in some way beyond the ordinary. We may not have to walk away from our job or family but no doubt Jesus thirst for your love and response.

Biography

Jerry is a happily married practicing Catholic, living in Central Massachusetts (New England, USA). He is actively involved in a variety of both doing and being ministries. To be present to both Jesus and others is his most difficult challenge in faith, as it is opposite to his nature of taking action. He could not do so if he did not take time for prayer. In all honesty, his life experiences in faith far outweigh a formal graduate degree in pastoral ministry. His observation is that this formal education along with the scientist /engineer /manager, and his doubting Thomas within, appropriately mingles the human and divine nature of who he is. He has found the he quickly burns out if he attempts to fight every single wrong he observes.

Jerry has realized that his specific commission means he must responsibly identify and use his God given gifts. He tries to share his belief in our loving Trinity in as appropriate way as possible, especially the moments of accepting Jesus's will. He loves to write of the ordinary times of God's peace, love, and actions. He strongly believes we are already participating in the mystery of heaven and eternity. He understands some of what he writes will be different from others beliefs as he does lean on his experiences and background as a Catholic. He only asks that you think ecumenically and let the Holy Spirit regulate your reaction to simply accepting another person's belief that has the commonality of "God is love."

Jerry prays that together we can Sing Joyfully to the Lord, as David does in Psalm 81.